T0311218

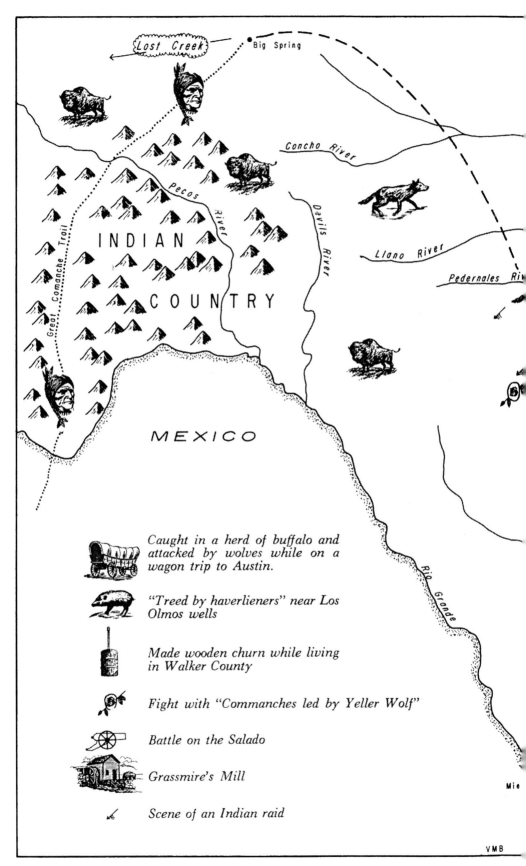

Lost Creek

Big Spring

Concho River

Pecos River

Devils River

Llano River

Pedernales Riv

Great Comanche Trail

INDIAN

COUNTRY

MEXICO

Rio Grande

Mie

Caught in a herd of buffalo and attacked by wolves while on a wagon trip to Austin.

"Treed by haverlieners" near Los Olmos wells

Made wooden churn while living in Walker County

Fight with "Commanches led by Yeller Wolf"

Battle on the Salado

Grassmire's Mill

Scene of an Indian raid

VMB

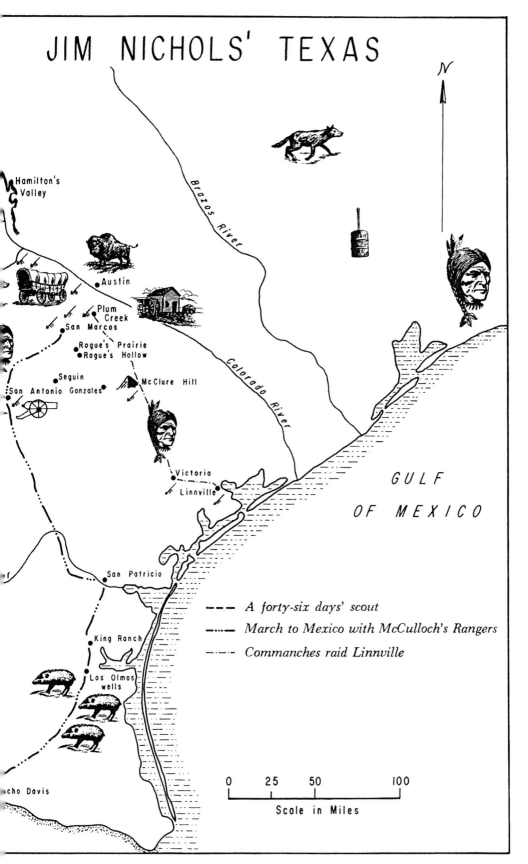

NOW YOU HEAR MY HORN

The Journal of James Wilson Nichols

1820–1887

Now You Hear My Horn

The Journal of
James Wilson Nichols
1820-1887

EDITED BY

CATHERINE W. McDOWELL

ILLUSTRATED BY

ELDRIDGE HARDIE

UNIVERSITY OF TEXAS PRESS : AUSTIN & LONDON

Library of Congress Catalog Card No. 66–15698

Design and Typography

ISBN 0-292-75582-1

It seems to me much better to read a man's own writing than to read what others say about him.

GEORGE ELIOT, *Life and Letters*

FOREWORD

One saturday in november of 1962 a thirteen-year-old girl, Sylvia Peters, came into the Daughters of the Republic of Texas Library at the Alamo and handed the Librarian, Miss Carmen Perry, a tightly rolled sheaf of papers, saying it was the journal of her great-great-grandfather James Wilson Nichols. He had been a butcher at the Alamo, she said, and was one of those who went out to find more beeves but then could not return because the Mexican army had encircled the Alamo.

The realization that perhaps here was a new name to add to the list of those men who had been at the Alamo was so exciting that Miss Perry asked Sylvia to leave the journal so we could read it. The torn, stained, insect-damaged papers unrolled into such a fresh, vivid account of the experiences of one of the pioneers of Texas and his associates that they were immediately recognized as a valuable contribution to primary-source material on Texas history, worthy of publication whether connected with the Alamo or not. Inspection of the manuscript showed some pages badly torn and faded and others missing. From members of the Nichols family we learned that the papers had passed through many hands and that pages could have been removed or lost, for the Journal had been valued by some but not by others. Also, parts had been given to persons outside the family to be published and apparently not returned.

Jim Nichols tells us that from the time he was twelve years old he kept journals or diaries, and that this story was written from these records, not from memory alone. While he does not give a date for writing the Journal, he does refer to events that took place in 1844 as happening "forty-three years ago," which would make 1887 the year he wrote the book. He was then sixty-seven years of age.

A new country needs its heroes but it must have plain folk, too. Those who daily contend with man, beast, land, and weather —the enemies of pioneers. Such plain folk were the Nichols family.

Passage over she traveled with me the rest of the way down
when we arived there was a scooner ready to sail she
bid me farewell thanking me for my kindness and entered
the boat I loaded my wagon and started out it was then
near sundown I was near two miles on my way but had about
three more to make to git water and grass I looked back and
saw her coming in a trot she waved her bundle and I sto-
-ped thinking may be she has forgoten something she came up
and said the captain would not take her in to work her passa-
-ge and now said she I want to go back home with you I
taken her back home and her and her husband lived to get
her untill they raised a large family of children and
her untill I withhold her name as she is still lizeing and

Eastern Texas getting married, an old Church

a three dollar Colt 'S' "C" "McCulloch raises a company

treat by travelings

Company The Mexican War, a trip to Monterey. The

raid of Monterey in the Spring of 1843 the

Comanche Indians became very troublesome on the west

especially around San antonio John C. Hays applied to

the authorities at austin and procured an order to raise

a company of mounted rangers for twelve months

Travis Captain Turner Joe Williams John Rogers William

Deadmen James Roberts and myself joined him we was

stationed at the old Mission below San antonio "My

+ (bigfoot) Wallace was elected first Lieutenant and Ad

Gillshi Second we needed no more officers Trute with

the captain was to lead all Scouts I was chosen trailer

*James W. and Mary Ann Nichols
and Mary Ann Sylvanie, Their Youngest Daughter*
(c. 1870)

From the days of the American Revolution there were Nicholses fighting in wars and following the trails west. They went from South Carolina into Tennessee, where they stayed a generation; then in the 1830's they started west again. Down the Mississippi they came from Memphis to Grande Lake, Arkansas. A few years there and once more they were on the Mississippi to the mouth of the Red River, then up the Red River to Natchitoches, Louisiana, and overland to San Augustine, Texas, crossing the Sabine River into Texas on December 16, 1836. A few months later they were in the Gonzales-Seguin area, where they settled down.[1]

James Wilson Nichols' immediate family consisted of his grandfather David Nichols; his father and mother, George Washington and Mary Ann Walker Nichols; three brothers; and four sisters. In 1844 he married Mary Ann Daniell, daughter of the Reverend George Daniell, and they raised twelve children.[2] Three of their sons married three daughters of Milford Day,[3] who had come to Texas when the Nichols family did, and it is from descendants of these that much of our information about the Nichols family has come. The George Washington Nichols family and the Johnson Day family traveled from Arkansas to Texas together and always remained close to each other, taking

[1] We do not know if the Nichols-Day party went from San Augustine to Gonzales by the Camino Real (Old Spanish Trail) as far as the Guadalupe River and then turned southeast, or by San Felipe de Austin and then turned west. An 1836 *New Map of Texas* contained the following comment: "Remarks on Texas. The usual mode of visiting Texas is by sea, from New Orleans to Galveston . . . and by land, from Natchitoches by San Augustine, Nacogdoches, Trinidad river &c" (copy of this map is in D.R.T. Library, San Antonio).

[2] George Wilson Nichols, b. November 5, 1844; Solomon Grundy Nichols, b. June 27, 1846; Alexander Green Nichols, b. August 2, 1848; James Marion Nichols, b. July 6, 1851; John Daniell Nichols, b. September 1, 1853; William Roland Nichols, b. October 5, 1855; Maria Olive Nichols, b. November 4, 1857; Sam Houston Nichols, b. November 10, 1859; Joseph Franklin Nichols, b. May 6, 1862; Eustace Benton Nichols, b. June 12, 1864; Sebron Monroe Nichols, b. July 11, 1866; Mary Ann Sylvanie Nichols, b. June 10, 1868.

[3] George Wilson Nichols married Sarah Day; Alexander Green Nichols married Caroline Jane Day; William Roland Nichols married Meeky Ann Day. Members of the Nichols-Day families who furnished this information were Mrs. Thelma Nichols Simonds, Doss, Texas, and Mrs. Effie Wright Kliefoth, San Antonio.

up their land in the same area[4] and many members of the two families marrying each other.

Mary Ann Walker Nichols died in 1838 shortly after the family settled in the Seguin area, and in 1840 George Washington Nichols and Rachel Sowell (widow of John Sowell, Sr., the blacksmith of Gonzales) were married.[5] There is a delightful fragmentary account of their courtship in the Journal:

Asa Sowell was almost the only person, after his sister married, that could converse with his mother who was delicate and very deef. He had learned to talk to her by signes as the other boys ware almost constantly in the woods and his father at his anvil while he lived. The old man died in 1838 and the family mooved to Seguin whare they had a league and a labor of land near that place but not thinking it safe to occupy their land they baught property and settled in Seguin. My mother haveing died the same year 1838 and Father almost compeled to be away from home a great potion of his time after his stock or chaceing Indians and when I was not thare had to leave four girl children at home by themselves, he became disgusted at a widowers life and as the Widow Sowell was one of only two widows living in Seguin he undertook to court her. It was in the spring of 1840 that he taken this notion and he tried every plan that he could conceive to make her understand but failed in every effort. She was so deef he could not hollow in her ear for fear of being heard all over town and he fail to make her understand by his signes so he had to call on Asa to interpet for him. Asa done the courting for them and they married.

[4] Records of the General Land Office of the State of Texas, Austin, show the following: *File 52*: Gonzales County. 2nd Class Conditional Certificate No. 25. George W. Nichols. 1280 acres, October 18, 1838. *File 52*: Gonzales County. 2nd Class. Field Notes 1280 acres. G. W. Nichols. Situated in County of Caldwell on waters of Plum Creek about 15 miles above town of Gonzales. Surveyed 30th day of January, 1842. *File 52*: Gonzales County. 2nd Class. Unconditional Certificate No. 16 of Guadalupe County. George W. Nichols. 1280 acres by virtue of Certificate No. 25 of Gonzales County. Dated 11th day of October, 1847. *File 78*: Bexar County 2nd Class Conditional Certificate No. 42. Jas. M. Day, Administrator of the Estate of Johnson Day, deceased. 1280 acres of land. Issued by Gonzales County Board of Land Commissioners. 18th day of October, 1838.

Records of the County Clerk's Office, Gonzales County Courthouse, show: *Probate Records of Gonzales County*: Letters of administration for estate of Johnson Day, deceased, issued to James M. Day, August 27, 1838.

Copies of these records are in the D.R.T. Library, San Antonio.

[5] From Index to Marriage Licenses, Gonzales County, Texas, Vol. I (Gonzales County Courthouse, Gonzales): "George W. Nichols & Rachel S. Sowell, Marriage License No. 62. July the 31st, 1840. Recorded in Book Letter A in page 23. E. Williams."

Later they became involved in controversy over land that had belonged to John Sowell, Sr.,[6] and eventually were divorced.[7]

Like his father and grandfather, James Wilson Nichols frequently moved from one place to another, but he always returned to the Guadalupe-Gonzales counties area. He must have been a mighty restless man, for when he wasn't establishing a new home after a move he was off chasing Indians or fighting Mexicans. He fought the Indians as a member of the Jack Hays, Mathew Caldwell, and James Callahan companies of Rangers, Frontier Battalions, and Minute Men,[8] and left graphic descriptions of these experiences. He was with Caldwell during the Battle on the Salado against General Adrian Woll in 1842, and under Hays and McCulloch during the U.S.-Mexican War of 1846. Because he did not want to secede from the Union he became involved in many conflicts with Confederate sympathizers during the Civil War. He was a man of strong convictions and never hesitated to do or say what he believed, often to his regret. After a full and active life he died on October 8, 1891, in Kerrville, Texas,[9] four years after writing this story.

Many accounts have been written about these events, each differing in some way. Those who participated in them saw the action from personal locations and viewpoints and wrote accordingly; those who were not participants wrote versions from what they had been told by ones who did take part or from what they imagined. Being a participant, Jim Nichols told what he saw from where he was, and was rather pointed in disagreeing with accounts previously published. There is no misunderstanding his meaning when he says that some "have gone

[6] Records in the Guadalupe County Courthouse show evidence of a lawsuit concerning an attempt to transfer Sowell property to G. W. Nichols.

[7] Statement of Mrs. S. P. Bolles, San Antonio, who is a descendant of John Sowell, Sr., the blacksmith of Gonzales.

[8] The Texas State Library and Archives, Austin, records show: Claim of James Wilson Nichols for service in the Woll Campaign, dated September 2, 1854; authorization for payment of Claim for Service in the Woll Campaign of 1842, dated July 2, 1855; pension payments to Jas. W. Nichols for 1856, 1857, 1859, 1861. Copies of these records are in the D.R.T. Library, San Antonio.

[9] Information furnished by members of the Nichols family.

beyond their own abilities in the performance even to pervert plain facts" and, later, "Chin music goes a long ways with some of the late writers."

Nor does Nichols' version always agree with the official reports of these affairs, and this is understandable, for the comprehensive viewpoint and the limited, personal one frequently differ. During World War II, soldiers who read official accounts of a battle often did not recognize the broad action described as one in which they had participated, for they knew only what had taken place in the one small sector where they had been located.[10]

Nothing in the manuscript verifies the family story that Jim Nichols was one of those who went out from the Alamo to get provisions and that before he could return, the Mexicans made their final assault and the Alamo fell. We made an all-out search for information about James Wilson Nichols, and from all we have learned we must conclude he was not at the Alamo. The manuscript states that the Nichols family crossed the Sabine River into Texas on December 16, 1836, which would have made it impossible for Jim Nichols to have been in San Antonio from February 23 to March 6, 1836, when the Alamo was under siege. The Second-Class Headright issued to Geoge Washington Nichols, Jim Nichols' father, indicates the family arrived in Gonzales after March 2, 1836. When Jim Nichols tells of going, at a later date, to San Antonio with his father and Johnson Day and of seeing David Crockett's gun and, a year or two later, his cap, he makes no reference to having been there before or to having ever seen Crockett himself. Yet, from the way he wrote of other experiences, one would think that he would have said something about it if he had known Crockett previously.

However, since the story of his having been at the Alamo comes from descendants who have not known each other and whose only mutual ancestors are Jim Nichols and Milford Day, it must have some basis, to have been handed down in all branches of the family. We know that Andrew Sowell, Byrd Lockhart, and some others did leave the Alamo in search of pro-

---

[10] Personal observation of the writer during World War II.

visions and that Sowell and Lockhart were from the Gonzales area, where the Nichols family settled. We also know that Jim Nichols' sister, Elizabeth, married John Sowell, Jr., and that his father, George Washington Nichols, married Rachel Sowell, the mother of John and Andrew Sowell, shortly after the two families moved to Guadalupe County, thus making Jim Nichols and Andrew Sowell both brothers-in-law and stepbrothers. In the telling through the years these two could have been confused. There was a close relationship between the two families through the marriages, but in later years animosities and jealousies developed, and somehow the Journal became involved— how, the missing pages of this manuscript would probably tell.

In preparing the manuscript for publication, great care has been taken to preserve the original choice of words and spelling and to add punctuation only where it was needed to clarify meaning. In those places where sentences or paragraphs are missing we have tried to convey what Jim Nichols evidently intended to say. All his chapter headings have been retained even though the accounts describing some of them are missing, for the headings are indicative of events in Nichols' life, and it was felt they might be instrumental in bringing to light some of the missing parts of the manuscript.

Many people have had important parts in making this book possible. Mrs. Ella K. Daggett Stumpf, a member of the Alamo Mission Chapter of the Daughters of the Republic of Texas, purchased the manuscript and gave it to the D.R.T. Library in memory of her mother, Mrs. Ella Ketcham Daggett. But there would not have been any manuscript to purchase if Mrs. Flora Chamberlain Nichols had not taken care of it for so long a time before she passed it on to her granddaughter, Sylvia Peters, and if Sylvia had not appreciated its contents and brought it to the D.R.T. Library.

How could any of us ever forget the day Mrs. Effie Kliefoth walked into the Library seeking information about her great-grandfather James Milford Day, so that she could become a member of the Daughters of the Republic of Texas, and when asked if she knew the name "Jim Nichols," said, "If you mean James Wilson Nichols, he was another great-grandfather."

Pictures of Mr. and Mrs. James W. Nichols and of James Milford Day were obtained through Mrs. Thelma Nichols Simonds, a granddaughter of both Jim Nichols and Milford Day. Miss Ella Jandt of Seguin searched the Guadalupe County records for everything, from maps showing Jim Nichols' property location to his cattle brand. Mr. Robert Boothe and the personnel of the County Clerk's Office in Gonzales County were so helpful in locating information we sought there that we were able to get copies made and be on our way back to San Antonio in three hours. Mr. James M. Day, Mrs. Mary Osburn, and all the staff of the Texas State Archives in Austin accepted periodic one-day forays into their domain with graciousness, and patiently provided material to answer "impossible" questions. Mr. Robert Stephens and Mr. David B. McFadden, U.S.-Mexican War buffs, and the staff of the San Antonio Public Library gave valuable information on Nichols' Mexican War service, "The Maid of Monterrey," and Arista's Gardens.

Mrs. Joyce Kunz Albaugh, a D.R.T., performed the tremendous task of transcribing the original manuscript to typewritten copy, and Mrs. Jacqueline Runnels Espy, also a D.R.T., gave many early-morning hours to reading background material, helping corroborate the authenticity of the events Nichols described, and typing.

Miss Carmen Perry, Librarian of the D.R.T. Library, cheerfully took on the additional work created by my involvement with "Jim Nichols" and was my strongest prop. To all these and all who gave my ego a boost when I most needed it, I am sincerely grateful.

Many pages of many books have been read, many letters have been written, many questions have been posed—and not all answered. Now, four and a half years later, here is the book.

San Antonio, Texas
1967

CATHERINE W. McDOWELL

CONTENTS

ILLUSTRATIONS

Life and Adventures
of an
Old Texas Ranger

*Written by Himself with a Concise Account of All the
Campaigns and Battles in which He partisapated with a
Thrilling Account of Personal Adventures and Encounters
from Early Boyhood to Mature Age and the Lives of Some
of the Most Noted Officers that he Served under and with.*

James W. Nichols' Cattle Brand

(Guadalupe County Records, Seguin, Texas)

PREFACE

Those who write books, dont I perceive, take the trouble on one and the same account but for many reasons and those reasons such as are very different. For some of them apply themselves to that part of learning to show their great skill in composition and tharein acquire a reputation for writeing finely, and others thare are who write books in order to gratify those that hapen to be concerned in them or the friends or relatives of those they write about, and on that account have gone beyond their own abilities in the performance even to pervert plain facts.

But thare are others who of necessity are driven to write history becase they themselves ware concerned in the facts so perverted and so cannot excuse themselves from committing them to writeing for the benefit of posterity. Now of these many reasons for writeing this little book I profess the last given reason for I was myself interested in that war between Texas and Mexico, the border wars with the Indians, and I saw other writers perverted the facts of history, and another reason though I have for writeing this book is to bring to light some interesting incidences which I myself was concerned with and which has never found thier way into the public prints. This work is not written from memory but from a memorundum or note book which I have kept from the time I was twelve years old.

AUTHOR.

[1887]

INTERDUCTION

🙟 In INTERDUCEING this little work for the benefit of the rising generation of the connection who may wish to know of their foreparents, I will state that the Nichols were of England but in an early day came to the United States, and when the Revolution broak out my great grandfather, Solomen R. Nichols, raised a company for that war, and he was killed at the head of his company at the Battle of Lundays Lane.[1] He left 4 sons the youngest of which was my grandfather, David Nichols, who married and lived in Charleston, South Carolina whare my father George Washington Nichols was born.

Then [they] emegrated to Frankling County, Tennessee, but before the county was organized, and settled at Pond Spring and at that time owned the land whare Winchester now stands. While living thare my father married Mary Ann Walker and she bore him four sons, Solomon G., Thomas R., and John W., and the writer, and in the Indian War of 1812 and 13 my father commanded a company and was wounded in the knee at the Battle of the Horseshoe Bend which made him a cripple for life.

In 1815 he again inlisted and was in the battle at New Orleans and saw General Packenham stowed away in a hogshead of rum and shiped for interment in his native land. It was said that the soldiers bored gimblet holes in the hogshead drew out the rum and drank it and the boddy was so decomposed that they was compeled to burry the hogshead with the remaines in it. Brother Thomas R. Nichols was born the day of the battle, the 8th day of January 1815, and I was the 4th son but the 5th child.

---

[1] The Battle of Lundy's Lane took place on July 25, 1814, in Canada, near Bridgewater and Niagara Falls. Americans were under Generals Jacob Brown and Winfield Scott, the British under Generals Riall and Drummond. The fighting was protracted and savage, with both sides claiming the victory, but the British remained in possession of the field. See Thomas C. Cochran and Wayne Andrews, eds., *Concise Dictionary of American History*, 1962, p. 577.

Route of Nichols Family to Texas in 1836

TENNESSEE

ARKANSAS

Memphis

Miss. River

Grande Lake

Miss.

INDIAN TERRITORY

Natchitoches

LOUISIANA

New Orleans

Red River

Sabine River

San Augustine

GULF OF MEXICO

Braxos River

Colorado River

Gonzales

Guadalupe River

T E X A S

San Antonio

Rio Grande

MEXICO

•••••• Route of Nichols family into Texas

‒‒‒‒ Probable route through Texas

CHAPTER I

Birthplace of the Writer and
Incidents and Occurences in His Boyhood

I WAS BORN in Franklin County, Tennessee, whare Win-chester stands on the 27th day of December, 1820, and my father and grandfather mooved from thare to the western district of the same state, Madison County, when I was quite small and lived thare five years. My father and grandfather decided to moove west and built themselves a flat boat and floated down the Tennessee River to the mouth and launched out on the Father of Watters, the Mississippi, and floated to Memphis when thare was but one store in the place run in the firm name of Byas and Moore. We then crossed over to High Point and stayed thare in camp through the winter useing driftwood for fuel.

I was about nine years old then and I could manage a small skiff very well and caught nearly all the driftwood we burned but come near loosing my life at one time and it was in this wise. My father and all the older boys was absent on buizness and I saw a prime drift log floating down, and ran to my skiff, jumped in and pulled toward the log, drove a spike in it and was just pulling for shore when I discovered a large steamboat huging the point and makeing directly between me and the shore. Now the waves that a large steamboat makes will sink a large skiff and my situation was perilous. My mother screamed and holled untill she suceeded in arousing the boats crew and one of them jumped into their skiff and got to me a few minutes after my skiff capized, but I held on to the log untill he reached me and he then carried me and the log all safe to shore and I never risked another skiff for a drift log when thare ware a steamboat near and I always looked before I leaped after that. In the spring we mooved out on Grande Lake.

It was quit common for people them days to take raft timber to New Orleans and sell it, and the way they would do this they would go into the large cypres breaks in the dry season, cut the

nice long trees, and chop them off as long as they could git them
good. Som of these logs would be two hundred feete long, others
only one hundred feete and they would cut two, three, four hundred of these logs and call it a raft. When the overflow of the
Mississippi would come and fill up all low land or swamp with
back watter, they would go in thare and float out their logs, splice
them togeather, make a raft, turn them loose in the current and
float them down the river to market, and sometimes they would
load these rafts with hoop poles, staves, shingles, pumkins, corn,
potatoes or any kind of produce they wished to market.

One spring Father had one of these rafts cut and the time
come for him to raft the logs togeather and the river was riseing
rapidly when the boys older than me and som hired hands
started to raft the logs togeather. Father stayed one or two days
on som business and when he got ready he mounted a fine mare
he had, taken me behind him to bring the mare back and started
for his raft camp about fifteen miles.

We had five or six sloughes to cross and Father said we must
hurry up or they would be swiming before we could reach
them. We got to the first one and it looked full, and Father set
me down on the bank to try his mare to see if she would swim.
Well, she did not like the fun at first but after Father ducked her
head under a few times and got her ears full of watter she rose
swiming like a duck. Never did I see her equal in swiming
after that and she swam six of those sloughs, som of which was
several hundred yards accross them.

We come to the lowland or swamp whare his timber was cut
which was near a mile wide and on the other side of which was
the raft camp. We put in and sometimes the mare was in swiming watter for som distance and then she would touch bottom
and we mad it to camp wet and cold. It was too late for me to
return that night so I stayed til morning and the watter still riseing.

Next morning Father says to me, "Jim, do you think you can
go home today?"

I says, "I could if I could see the blazes on the trees, but the watter has covered up all the marks this morning and I am liable to miss the way."

Father says, "If you will do as I tell you thare is no danger and if you will not git scared and give the mare the briddle she will take you home safe."

I says, "I shal not git scard." I started and it was swiming watter for a little over a mile, then the mare come out on the ridg in the road and I believed what Father had told me. I let her blow for she was nearly exhausted and after resting a half hour I resumed my journay. I swam several miles that day and got home that evening to meete the most ancious mother and sister that ever lived.

I recon Father got his raft redy to start and he loaded it with cord wood and told Mother he was going to take me with him. Father had been on two or three such trips before but she objected at first but finely gave her consent and we cut loose one morning and floated down the river. Every steamboat would shy round us as the raft is master of the watters, but we would once in a while git into an eddy and whirl round and round awhile, but the hands managed to git out without much delay. I have known a raft to remain in an eddy for a week but we was not bothered much in that way, and we arrived safe in New Orleans and sold out for a good prise. The raft and its load sold for the prise of nine hundred dollars.

Father had a cousen, Terry Nichols, living in the city at the time and we had been thare just a week when Father said to his cousen, "I want to start home in the morning."

The next morning we all went down on the levy and was sitting thare waiting for a steamboat to unload her cargo as we was going up on her. It was awful hot and all at once Father fell over screeming with pain. Terry called a cab and the cabman and Terry lifted Father in to the cab and Terry told the cabman whare to go and started of in a run for a doctor. The cab and the doctor arived about the same time and the doctor said it was a sever case of colrea.

Terrys house was a large brick building seven stories high

and the doctor told Terry to have Father carried to the upper story and throw open all the doors and windows so he could git all the fresh are he could. Terry put us all in the elevater and we was hoisted, and finely got the cramping stoped but he lay thare for five days unconcious, but in a few more days he revived a little and after staying up in the seventh story of that house nine weeks and three days we once more went down and out on the levy to make a start for home, but this time sad, sorry and low spirited. Father had got his cousen to write home for him two or three times during his sickness but heard nothing from home, however, we got home safe and found nearly all the family sick but all anciously waiting and looking for us.

About this time the country being thinly settled and varmonts so numerous, bears, wolves, panthers, etc., that it was all most imposable to raise hogs in the woods. When we first settled thare Father went to a neighbor, Ben Louis, to buy some meat and a start of hogs, he had a fine lot of hogs.

Father says, "Mr. Louis, this country must be good for hogs, is it not?"

"Well, sir, it is the best hog country I ever lived in in my life if it was not for the insects."

"What kind of insects bothers hogs here, Mr. Louis?"

"O, its beares, painters, wolves and cats."

So after we had been thare a year or two the neighbors for miles around apointed a day and they drive the country through with hounds for these insects. Father had baught us boys all a good gun a piece and on one of these ocaisions thare was to be a big drive and all of the men but three or four would take stands along whare the main trailes crossed the big road so as to have an open place to see the ground and a cleare place to shoot. It was a thick timbered country and those three or four men would take the hounds and go back som miles to start the game. The morning came and it was all bustle and glee and I asked Father whare he was going to let me stand.

I says, "I want a good station."

"Well," said he, "I am going to station you at the plow handles."

I was near twelve years old but I could not help crying but thare was no use in talking and I had to take a horse and scuter ploe and break up a patch to sow turnips and I went to my work, Father and the other boys to their stands. I worked on until I had a few rounds to go to finish up my task when I heard the dogs let all holts go and I stoped and listened and they seemed to be comeing directly towards me but soon turned and went out of hearing. I thought maybe they would come back again so I ran to the house and got my gun, set it in the fence corner and went to plowing again. In a few minutes I heard the dogs break out again and I stoped and listened and they seemed to come nearer and I ran to my gun and on and on the dogs come nearer and nearer.

There was a trail ran along on the outside of the fence and about ten steps of. On they come and I knew they was in that trail but what they ware after I did not know and I thought it might be a beare, a panter or some other ferocious animil, and it might be a deer but I was safer inside the fence at any rate. I put my gun on the fence and made ready to shoot whatever it was, and still on they come. About sixty yards ahead of the dogs I saw a hugh buck come bounding along the trail and he got oposite me, stoped, threw his head round to look back and I leaveled my gun and fired. To my great joy he fell and I got over the fence but I could not tell you how I did it. I might have climbed over or jumped over or I might have fell over, but at any rate when I got to the deer the dogs had covered it and I had a hogkilling time gitting them off. I stood gazeing at my prize for some time thinking how will I get him round to the house. My ball had taken efect in his head although I supose my aim was at his boddy. I let the fence down, taken the singletree of the plow, taken one of my lines and tied round the deer hornes, hitched my horse to it and draged it round to the house.

Father and all the boys come in soon after all without meat and you bet they whooped me up until if I had been weighed that evening and had failed to pull down at least two hundred pounds I should have said, "Well, them steel yards is not corect!"

At another time the next spring the bufalo gnats was so bad

they seemed to be running all kinds of stock crazy and we kept old logs burning all the time to keep smokes for the stock to stand by, and these smokes was a good place to kill deer and other game at. One morning Father told me to go down in the switch cane and build som new smokes and mend up the old ones. I taken my gun and went down into the break and found a nice large dry log. It did not touch the ground in the middle by 8 or 10 inches and I had som fire and was down kindleing it up and started a little smoke when I heard something on the oposite side of the log rubing and snifing and grunting til it reached the smoke and I bent down to look under the log and thare was a huge old bare smokeing himself and I could have taken either of

his legs in my hand if I would, but you can bet high that I did not do it. I snatched up my gun and tried to shoot under the log but it was too low, and then I raised up and tried to shoot over the log but it was too high as the bare was against it, and I then ran to the but of the log but the smoke hid him and I could not see how to shoot him from thare, so I mounted the log and walked up to whare he was, put the musel of my gun within two inches of his head and fired.

I dont know whether I could have hit the side of a house ten steps or not I was trimbling so but at any rate I spattered his braines against the log. I ran back to the house yelling and the boys went back with me and taken the oxen and cart to bring in the meat. I dont know how much I would have weighed that evening had I been weighed acording to my feelings of the big man that I thought I was.

That summer I was bitten by a large rattlesnake and came near dying and about the time I got well old John M. Peepeles came into the settlement and taken up school and I went to school. Three monts was all the scooling I ever got but the teacher boarded with Father the three months out and I made such progress in my studdies that the teacher taken a likeing to me and taught me at school in day time and till late at night at home.

Father told him how many narrow escapes I had up to that time and he told me I aught to keep a memorandom of all the noted incidences and if my after life was as eventful as my early life I would be able to write an interesting book when I got old, and I commenced to keep a journel of my life noting down all the incidences as they would ocur and kept it up and now I write from this memorandom book or journal. Thare are many things noted down in my journal of miner importance which I shal not mention in this work becase it would make it too large and teadious.

CHAPTER II

Mooving to Texas. Catching a Large Fish. Mooveing to Gonzales County. The First Rangeing Co. False Alarm. Indian Raid. Going to Mill. Attacted by Wolves, etc.

IN THE SUMMER of 1836 Father sold out in Arkansas to moove to Texas and his destination was San Antonio, but about a week before we was ready to start one evening som moovers drove up and baught som corn and fodder from Father and drove out and camped. After supper Father went out to the camp to chat and find out whare they was mooveing to and I went with him and we found out that their names was Day and that they was mooveing to Texas. This was Johnson Day and family, Milfords father, and Father and old man Day mad a covenent that night to git togeather, travil togeather, and settle togeather. It seemed to suit som of both families as thare was several grown children in both families, and thare was two matches mad up on the way. We got with Day and traveled togeather all the way and crossed the Sabine River into Texas the 16th day of December 1836, and mooved on out to San Augustine and rented land from old man Richards.

The winter was so severe that in climeting our oxen all died but one yoak. We was obliged to have oxen as they would work on the range and we could procure no forage for horses, so Brother John and myself went down on the Antholine River and baught three or four yoak of wild beeves from John Thorn[1] to breake and make a crop with, and while I was thare I caught the largest fish I ever saw before or since.

While Brother John was workeing with the steers I concluded to catch som fish, I had som large cat hooks with me such as I had been fishing with in the Irish Buyo and I set som of them out one night and next morning all my hooks was broken and

---

[1] Nichols must mean the Angelina River; John S. Thorn's land was in Nacogdoches County. See *Abstract of Valid Land Claims of the State of Texas*, compiled by John Burlage and J. B. Hollingsworth (Austin: John Marshall & Company, 1859), p. 521. Copy of this book is in D.R.T. Library, San Antonio.

Thorn soon told me that the store baught hooks would not stand the fish in that river. I went to the shop and had me a hook mad and baited it with a whole rabbit, set it out, and next morning I went to my hook, and it had caught what I turmed a large fish and another larger one had come along and swallowed it above its side fins and hung, and I could not take them out of the watter. I went back to the house and got Mr. Thorn and a negro man, both large stout men, and they taken them out of the watter, tied a rope in ones mouth, put a pole in the loop and shouldered it up and at least a foot of the large one draged the ground.

The large one weighed 107 pounds, the small one 49 pounds, so I caught 156 pounds of fish at one time and on one hook. Thorn said he had caught one larger than that since he lived thare, and now dear reader, if you are inclined to dout this wolf story about the big fish, I cant help it for I believe the witnesses are all dead and the papers destroyed except my memorandon book. We got our steers so we could manage them and went home.

After this Brother Solomon and I taken a contract to haul som hay to town for som parties as Brother John and Milford was freighting, and while hauling the hay I mad the acquaintence of Judg John A. Quitman, afterwards General Quitman, so noted in the Mexican War. The judg was in camp thare with 15 or 16 companions on a prospecting tour and I was at his camp often and got pretty well acquainted with him and the most of his men, and they all baught hay from me nearly every trip I mad.

We finished up our job and not long after this Father and Day began preperations to moove west. We mad the trip to Gonzales and stoped thare but Father and Day had never abandond the notion of going to San Antonio before they stoped and now concluded to first go and look before they mooved thare. Father had heard so much about old San Antonio in his early life he wanted to see the place.

Thare was a croud going out and Brother Solomon and I went with them. While thare I found a Mexican with old Davy Crockets gun and it was broak off at the bretch and it was a very noted gun. The naked barrel weighed 18 pounds with a plate of silver

let into the barrel just behind the hind sight with the name Davy
Crockette ingraved on it and another plate near the bretch with
Drue Lane make[2] ingraved on it, and thare was a young man
with us claimed to be a son of Davy Crocketts baught the gun
and carried it off home.

A year or two after that I was in San Antonio and found Crocketts cap mad out of a rackoon skin with the hair pulled out leaving only the fur and with a fox tail hanging down behind, also
his shot pouch mad of panter-skin with the tail for a flap. I told
Father about it and he wrote to Bob Crockette, Mempis, Tennessee, but never got an answer, and I saw them once after that but
I could not buy them.

Father and Day decided not to moove to San Antonio and returned to Gonzales. John and Milford, thinking the old folks
would settle somewhare in the county, them and their girls was
gitting ancious to marry, and concluded to do so, but thare was
no regular mode of marrying in vogue, the licens law not yet
being established. Under the Constitution of 1824 thare still remained a mode of marrying by bond[3] whare the parties bound
themselves to live togeather as man and wife a certain lenght of
time, then they could renew their bond or go free, and the same
mode is the costom in Mexico now. Milford and John married
their girls, Milford married my sister Martha, my oldest sister,
and John married Polly Day, Milford's oldest sister, under that
law for a certain length of time and when that time ran out they
seemed to git along well and liked the fun so they entered on
another six months probation. By the time that ran out the licens
law was established and still they cleaved to each other and taken
out licens[4] and married right and lived togeather as long as lives
lamp held out to burn. Milfords wife died first but he is still living, and Brother John died and his wife is still living.

[2] Have been unable to verify this make of gun.

[3] "An Act Legalizing and Confirming Certain Marriages Therein Named," in
Laws of Texas, 1822–1897, compiled by H. P. N. Gammel (10 vols., Austin: Gammel Book Company, 1898), II, 640.

[4] Index to Marriage Licenses, Gonzales County, Texas, Vol. I (Gonzales County
Courthouse, Gonzales, Texas).

Soon after we returned from San Antonio the Indians mad a raid and stole som horses and Joe B. Clements raised a small company of nineteen men, and Brother Thomas and I joined his company. We held ourselves in readyness to go when caled on, and later on the Indians mad another raid, stole som horses, and Captain Clements being sick, seven or eight of us started in persuit with old Uncle Dan Davis, who was an old setler and had som experience in fighting Indians. We followed on the trail about fifteen miles and lost the trail and in scatering to hunt the trail we lost Uncle Dan. We whooped and hollowed and shot of guns and waited som two hours but we heard nothing of him nor did we find the trail, and we concluded to return and was until after night gitting back, but when we got thare we found the town all in confusion, comotion and forted up.

Now I will mention the most of the men who had families thare at that time. Dan Wash and Jack Davis, Zeke and French Smith, Adam Zumalt, my father, John Sowell, Francis Berry, John Clark, Eli Mitchel, Ed Ballinger, Jim Jipson, Joe Clements, Miles Dykes, and Ben Duncan, Johnson Day, Milford Day, John Nichols, and the single men was Anson Neill, John Archer, Arch Jones, Arch Gipson, Bill and Mike Cody, Zeke Williams, C. C. DeWitt, Dave Durst, Andrew and John Sowell, Ed Milloch, Solomon and Thomas Nichols and others.

It apears when old Uncle Dan got lost from us on the Indian trail he got crazy and started for home and he too was after dark gitting in, but his horse was run down, so he had to walk and lead him the last mile or two. He reported the wood full of Indians and he had seen, he said, five or six hundred and they was all painted, som red, som black and all naked. Well, he had always been such a truthful man the people believed him and they sent out, got all the women and children and forted up with all the men on the outside, guns in hand. After a while John Archer and myself was put on guard. We expected to be attacted and layed our plans accordingly, and about midnight the attact comenced but not by Indians.

Old Man Zumalt had a big fine sow and a great favorite. The night was very dark and the old sow concluded the horses had corn and she would devide with them and she was makeing that way when Archer saw her bulk and, he said afterwards, he thought it was three Indians, one after another, on all fores. He squated down low to git them in range and fired and the bulk fell but thare was no attact made. We got a light and found what he had done, he had kiled the old sow, and we mad such a nois and fuss it awoke Uncle Dan whare he had gone to sleepe and he came out raving, mad cursing and swaring, and no boddy had ever heard him sware before. [He] shot of his gun and hollered, "Now, you have done it!"

"Done what, Uncle Dan?" someone suggested.

"Why, let the Indians git away," said he. "I had them all in the pen and now you have let them all out."

"I did not see any Indians," said one.

"Why, don't you see them on top of yon house? Som is going up feet formost. Look!" said he, "yonder is a thousand."

We began to see that he was crazy and that his first alarm was from amagenation while in a fit of insanity, and that broak up the fort.

It was not long after this the Indians mad a raid on the setlements and stole som horses. Old Man Zumalt had a good horse in his stable built of logs, and the Indians tried the door but it was locked and they shot arrows through the cracks till they kiled the horse. They collected up a small drove of horses and started of but [found] Zeke Williams horse hobbled out with a pare of iron hobbles. They could not cut the hobbles nor take them of but they kiled the horse, cut his legs of at the knees and taken legs, hobbles and all, of with them,[5] evidently to learn the combination and how to take them of if they should ever find such on other horses.

In these early days there was no mills to grind corn, that article so scarce thare was not much use for mills, and the nearest mill

---

[5] A. J. Sowell also recounts this happening in his *Incidents of History in Guadalupe County* (Seguin, Texas: C. L. Martin, Publisher, n.d.), p. 18: "One of the settlers thinking to outwit the Indians, procured a pair of iron hopples [sic] and locked them on his horse's legs. Not long afterwards the Indians made a raid and drove nearly all of the horses out of the valley. Next morning the horse which wore the iron hopples was found dead, his feet cut off and the hopples gone."

was Grassmires on the Colorado River,⁶ distant near 70 miles, and only a few steel hand mills. It was understood that thare was plenty of meal to sell at that mill, so Father and Old Man Sowell and one or two others mad up money to buy a load of meal and Father agreede to furnish the wagon and one yoak of oxen and a driver, if others would furnish money to buy his meal and they agreede. Old Man Sowell agreede to furnish so much money, one yoak of oxen and a boy to help drive and for company, and it was agreed that myself and Asa Sowell would go.

We roled out one morning, no signe of a road atal to travil the whole way, our oxen fat and unruly, and the first day powerful hot. We went on and crossed Peach Creek about 4 oclock and thare we rested about one hour, and not knowing whare we would git the next watter, we wattered our steers, filled up our goards, and started. It was cool that evening and we traveled fast and got about 8 miles from the creek, came to a brushy ridg, could not see how to pick our way through, and camped, hobbled out our oxen, eat our suppers, and went to sleepe. Next morning my oxen was in sight but the others we could not see, but I told Asa to go round and take a look for them while I mad som coffee, and he taken a big round but no oxen, and he came in and while he was eating I told him I would take a round. I thought I could find the trail and soon trail them up. Directly I struck their trail and could trail them easyly as the grass was high, and I troted on the trail about two miles and found their hobbles and I knew then they was gone a long way.

Then, I thought, Asa was young and scarry and I had better go back and git him so we would be togeather if anything should hapen as we never knew when thare was danger. I went back to the wagon and found Asa nearly scared to death as he had heard a gun fire in the direction that I had gone and he thought the Indians had attacted me, and as I had stayed so long, had kiled me, and he was turable uneasy. We then tied up my oxen, taken our guns and goards, then nearly emty, and struck out on the

⁶ F. W. Grassmeyer's land was in Fayette and Bastrop counties, as the county line ran through his property. Its eastern boundary was the Colorado River, according to a map of Fayette County, copyright 1879. Copy in D.R.T. Library, San Antonio.

trail of the oxen through the country nearly due north, and we followed on the trail til about sundown when Asa said he would have to rest. He said he was awful hungry and while he was resting I walked round to see if I could find a squrel, a rabit, or a bird for I was hungry too, as neither of us had ate anything since early morning but could find nothing to shoot and after traveling intil dark we camped but could still find nothing to shoot.

Next morning we resumed our journey and went on until near two oclock in the evening when we come to a larg trail about two days and nights old. I examined it and found it had been Indians with a larg drove of horses, and thare we lost the trail of our oxen, but we crossed the Indian trail and found our oxen trail, and at the same time found whare the Indians had kiled a buffalo and had cut some pieces out of it, but the buzzards and wolves had picked the bones clean. We went on a mile or two farther and found a buffalo that the Indians had wounded and had stragled of and died.

It was now about 4 oclock in the evening the second day out from the wagon and we are now out of watter and fearful hungry. We concluded to try a peace of the buffalo meat but it was turably swelled being dead about 3 days and nights in hot weather, and I knew it would be short, but hunger knows no difrence in tainted or short meat and good meat. I cut of a hunk and smeled it and Whew! It smell like ripe peaches. We pitched in and we roasted and eat until we was loaded down to our heels, and Asa put a hunk in his pocket. That accounted for game being so scarce as all kinds of game will run for miles away from an Indian trail. We went on trailing our oxen for a few miles farther and we both began to get awful thirsty but still kept on til Asa gave out and I was near in the same fix, and we sat down and rested a while, then went on and soon come to a deepe beaten trail, and I told Asa that trail led to watter. We quit the oxen trail and followed the old trail through a low flat post oak country with the prospect good for a long walk but, fortunately for us, we soon struck a deepe dry creek. The trail led up the bed of the creek and we followed up the creek half mile and found watter, and behold, thare stood our oxen too. After drinking and resting and then resting and drinking, we filled our gourds, catched our oxen and started for the waggon, at least 18 miles and the sun only about one hour high.

We traveled about two miles when Asa said he was sick and layed down and I tied the oxen to a tree and went back to whare he was, and he comenced to throw up and he heaved and up come about two pounds of buffalo meat and a sluice of watter, then som more meat and watter mixed. [He] lay still a few seconds then heaved up som more buffalo meat and watter, then taken another drink of watter, and by this time it was dark and Asa had emted his goard and I had taken two drinks out of mine, and I began to study the situation. My oxen at the wagon tied up two days and a night with the prospect good for one more night and another day without watter or grass, and me, then at least 15 miles from them with an auful sick companion, and I reached over and felt his pults and he had a high fever.

After lying still a few minutes he awoke up and asked for watter and I handed him my goard, his being emty, he drank it emty and layed down again but soon raised up and heaved again, and up come som more meat and watter, then som more watter thickened with buffalo meat, and Oh! such a purfum! You would have said, "Well, that man aught to have been burrid a week ago." He laid down and was soon sound asleepe and I lay down but could not sleepe, and in about an hour Asa awoke and asked for watter and I told him thare was not a drop in neither goard. He lay down again and groaned, "Oh, Lordy!" but did not lay long before he raised up and comenced throwing up watter thickened with meat, then buffalo meat and watter.

When he threw up everything only what belonged inside of him he lay down again and lay still about an hour, and then roused up and said, "Watter, watter, Oh for Gods Sake, a little watter."

It was a ground-hog case and I knew in the fix he was in he was bound to have watter or die before morning.

I says, "Asa, if you promace me that you wont die til I git back, I will go and git you som more watter, as dark as it is."

He said he would try so I scaned around the place to see if I

would know it again in the dark, jest then the thought struck me
to build up a fire and I could see it a long ways, but thare was a
great draw back, the grass was tall and dry. I looked round and
found a tolerable naked place and scraped away the grass the
best I could with my butcher knife and built a small fire and
started. I took the trail that we had traveled the evening before,
mad it to the creek prety well, but found it very dark in the bed
of the creek and groped my way up to the watter, filled both
goards, and struck out for camp. I made it within sight and the
light blinded me so I could hardly travel attal, and I had not
discovered the cause of so much light, but when I arrived in
about 80 yards I saw a new dificulty had arose.

While I was gone the wind had sprang up and had blown som
small coles and sparks into the grass, and it was burning at a fearful rate. Asa, Oh, whare was he? He was not dead by about 36
years and was up fighting fire like he was killing snakes a dime
a dozen whare they was plentyful. I ran as fast as I could and
piched in to save the oxen and faught hard and tried to fire
against it but it was no go. The wind was too high and the fire
ran under the oxen and they reared and piched and tried to
break the rope, but that was no go so they had to take the chance.
The fire burned under them and singed all the hair of their legs
and bellies so that in a few days the hide fell of in peaces or
patches from the size of a peace of saddle blanket or a mules eare
to the size of a store bill.

But again to my mutton. After I found that the fire had outrun
me and got away I hollowed for Asa but could not raise him and
I went in search of him, and Hunted and hollowed and hunted
in vain. I went back to whare we had first stoped and whare I
had left the goards and began to muse thus, "Well, while I was
gone Asa died and wolves draged him off or the fire has burned
over him and blackened him so I can not see him in the dark
and dence smoke, but I kept walking round trying to recognize
the place whare I had left him, all the time peereing through the
smoke and darkness. Not fare from the goards I saw him lying
flat on his face and I thought, just as I expected, dead, by Gran-
nie, but on going up to him I found him still breathing. He had

left of fighting fire and had started to see if I had come back, got
that fare and fell exausted in a fainting fit. I ran got a goard of
watter and wet his face and head and poured som in his mouth,
took my handkerchief, wet it and put it on his breast and kept
poreing watter on him til I emted one gourd but he was still un-
conscious. I must have worked with him one hour and he opened
his eyes and looked round sorter wild and I says, "Asa, here is
some watter, dont you want a drink."

He raised up and drank and says, "Where are we? Oh Lordy!"
and lay down again.

After taking the second drink he lay down and was soon snore-
ing gloriously and I lay down but thare was no sleepe for me.
I lay thare studying what an eventful trip we had had, and it not
half over, and wished myself back at home under my mamies
bed cracking peanuts. I was lying thare studying these things
over until about an hour before day I heard a gang of wolves
thare looce, howling not over forty yards distant and I jump up
and went for my gun, the first time I had thought of it since I
had returned with the watter and Oh! Cracky! It, of corse was
not thare.

I awoke Asa and asked him about our guns and he said when
the fire broak out he snatched up both guns, draped the shot-
pouch straps around them and hung them up in a tree and
pointed to the tree. Now, I had heard som fearful yarns about
wolves attacting people and it mad me feel sorter spotted behind
the eares, and I got the guns down and was so glad it mad me
say to Asa, "Bully for your sore toe if it never gits well."

By this time Asa had stagered to his feete and took his gun,
and the wolves kept comeing and howling until they got within
fifteen steps of us. We both fixt ourselves to shoot at the sam
time, and if they still advanced on us we was to take to a stoop-
ing tree which stood close by, and when they got close by enough
we both fired and both kiled his wolf and the other ran of. We
went and draged them up into camp, taken out their liver, and
roasted and eat them.

By this time day had begun to break and we started for the
waggon and mad it about one oclock, and my oxen looked—well,

I cant hardly describe them. Well—they looked like a shitepoke
after swallowing a live eel a dozen times and couldnot make him
stick. Not knowing whare we would find the next water, after
eating a hunk of bread and bacon, we hiched up and started.
We had a fine looking team to start with, one yoak half roasted
and the other so gant they would hardly make a shadow, but
we went on all the same and hapened to strike watter a little before sundown and camped for the night.

By this time Asa was all rite, and I teased him a little about
the fire gitting out the night before, and I told him I knew that
when I left for watter that he spread the coles out to roast his
hunk of buffalo meat he put in his pocket to eat, and the fire had
broke out that way, but he said that hunk got to stinking so bad
he threw it away, and that night I injoyed a good nights sleepe.

Next day we mad it to the mill and found the mill crouded
with about twenty waggon loads of corn. I told Asa that was
bully for us, thare would be plenty of tall corn to sell us a half
dozen loads if we wanted that much.

We found the Colorado River about a mile wide at that place
and we was now out of provision, we could git plenty of meal at
the mill but nothing else. By inquire I learned thare was a store
on the oposite side of the river whare we could git a little of anything we wanted, flower, molasses, bacon, tobaco and whiskey.
There was a tight small skiff but none would take the risk in
crosing. I told them I could go and they said if I would go they
would pay for all the provision I needed and give me five dollars
extra if I would fetch what they wanted. We agreede and I taken
jugs, sacks for shugar and coffee, and canteens and goards for
whiskey.

I jumped in the skiff but the drift was running without in-
termission at a fearful rate, that was what scared them all of,
but I pulled up the river at my lasure until I was near a half
mile and saw a little gap in the drift and scuted through, went
on to the store, got all thare was sent for, and mad it back with
about two gallons of fighting whiskey, at any rate they had not
had it mor than an hour until thare was five or six fights.

Thare was 8 or 10, all young men, but one old scool teacher, that had started out afoot on a prospecting tour. Thare was old Billy Mitchel, the scool teacher, and Barney Wilson, Jarrett Randle, John R. and Henry B. King, Bill and Green Counningham, and they was going west. When they found that we was going to Gonzales they wanted to go with us and said they would furnish all the grub and do all the cooking if we would have their valiece and blankets and we agreede, as they was all well armed and they had a fiddle, a fife, and one or two jews harps, and all that had no musical instruments was good singers. We had a fine time going back without anything to mar the peace or interfeare with pleasure except one lone incident.

The second morning homeward bound while I was eating breackfast, old man Mitchel said he would go and drive up the other yoak of oxen as one yoak was already thare and started, but somone sugested he had better take his gun, a little short understriker, that carried a buckshot, and he taken his gun, started of singing "The wildflowers scattred oer the plain," walked round the oxen, stooped down to unhobble them, and went to raise up. One of the steers mad a lung at him and hooked him down on his belley and he turned over to git up and the steer stradled him and stood over him so he could not git up nor moove his boddy, and he twisted his gun round and fired. The steers jumped and expected to see one fall soon, but when the old man got up the steer mad another lung at him, hiched his horn in the old mans broadcloth coat tail and tore it half in two, leaving the sleeves on his arms, stagered him back and he fell again, and the steer stradled him holding him down. His gun was now emty and he lay thare until I walked at least a hundred and fifty yards and the old man hollering every breath, "Run, Run."

CHAPTER III

A FORTY-SIX DAYS SCOUT

A Novel of Proveing Away A Horse. Lost Creek. Starveing For Watter and Suplied in a Mericulous Way. Gitting Lost. Death of Swift, Nickles, Symons. A fight With Indians. A Tired Down Animal. Carried Forty Miles by Indians in Four or Five Hours.

THE INDIANS at this time was very trublesom. About a year before the incident that I am about to relate I had roped a good horse away from the mustangs, a gentle saddle horse and kept him about six months, and he prooved to be a good racer as he beat every horse that he ran against. I had a big race soon to come of against a noted race horse made with Bob Hall for 5.00 dollars, and the day of the race Lewis Goodin, a noted gambler then liveing on the Colorado River, came over to the races with several others and I beat the race, and Goodin, learning the facts of how I came by the horse from som parties, claimed the horse and prooved him away from me, but I gave him up very reluctently for I did not believe that he had ever before seen the horse.

The Indians kept makeing raids stealing horses until I with several others found ourselves afoot. I had become so attached to Mustang Bill as I called him that I went over to Goodins and baught him back, giveing Goodin a hundred dollars for him when ponies could be baught for from 15 to 20 dollars a head.

I had not had him long when the Indians mad a raid [stealing a] larg bunch of horses, amongst them w[as Captain Ja]mes Callahans main saddle horse, and that seemed to make the Captain so mad he ordered every man that could git a good horse to git ready for a twenty days scout. He said he did not want any man to go on a sorry horse for he intended to follow them to their den, and thare was twentysix men got ready and we started out

for San Antonio to purchase suplies for the scout. We arived at
San Antonio and was purchesing our outfit when a croud of
men came round gassing and proffasying concerning the result
of the expedition and looking at our horses [and] when one of
the men, Henry Dunn, came round to my horse and after examining him for a few seconds says, "Boys, this is my horse. He
was stolen from me about two years ago."

I says, "Now, my friend, you are mistaken for once, for about
a year ago I caught that horse from the mustangs and one Lewis
Goodin claimed him, prooved him, and taken him of, and a few
months ago I baught him back."

Said he, "I don't care if you got him in Calafornia. He is my
horse, or not mine, he belongs to my little boy, and I can proove
him by twenty men in this town."

By this time thare was a big croud and nearly all of our croud
with the rest. Som says, "I would not give him up, Jim, he is
trying to steal him."

Dunn says, "Now, I will tell you what I will do to convince
you and your croud. I will turn him loose here in this c[roud
of hor]ses and men, and if he dont go [strate to my house and]
go in at the front door through the house and out at the back
door into the back yard whare he was kept three years, then he
is your horse and not mine, and if he does, you are not to require
me to proove him, but it has been two years since he mad a track
in my back yard and he may have forgotten the place, but I will
risk it."

The Captain says, "Do that, Jim, you will git to ride the horse
on the trip."

But I did not doubt Dunns earnestness and I taken of my rig-
gin, turned him loose and Dunn taken him by the mane, turned
him round with his head from his house, struck him on the rump
with his hand and says, 'Go git your dinner!'."

The horse started of in a fast walk, then in a trot, the whole
croud followed and saw him enter the house amongst the children, go through into the back yard.

The children comenced screaming and hollowing, "O Papa!
Here is Sanchoe come back agin!"

That settled it, I tried to buy him but that was no go. We lay over one day so I could buy a horse, and I had several offered to me that evening but none that I could risk on such a trip, but next morning a Mexican offered me one that we all decided would do, and I baught him and mad Dunn give me papers so I could git my money back from Goodin, and we started.

We went up the country to the Llano River and thare we struck the Indian trail, and Simon Cockrel who had been a prisnr with the Indians [for som yea]rs was our guide. Him, myself and Andrew Sowell was put ahead to trail becase we was all good traillers, and we went on and on until we struck the Collorado River high up near the mouth of the Concho or South Fork, thence on up to whare Colorado City now stands and whare the trail left the river and bore out towards the plains.

The Indians had camped about one day and night at Big Spring whare the station Big Spring is now located on the railroad, and our guide Cockrel said that was the last watter on the corse the Indians ware traveling until we struck Lost Creek on the plaines, unless we found watter at a spring on the side of a mountain near the edg of the plains som 80 miles distant. Captain Callahan, after camping thare that night, told Cockrel to take the trail, and after takeing all the watter we could carry we struck out on the trail.

We mad two auful hard days march and about noon the third day reached the mountain, but the spring had gone dry. We dug down but found no watter, and thare was not a drop of watter in the croud, having used the last that morning. We held a consultation to decide on what we should do, and Cockrel said the trail led in the direction of Lost Creek and thare was no watter nearer than that creek in that direction, and it would take us two days and a half hard riding to reach it, and it would take us two days and a half to go back to Big Spring, the last watter we had passed, and som said go on to Lost Creek.

Lost Creek is a marshy place, a seap spring, whare a person can go out into it on tuffs of grass and shake the whole surface for yards around, and has been thickly set in time with large timber, mostly ash, but it has all died and fallen down and nearly all rotten. The source covers near three acres of ground [and] runs togeather and makes a large pool or lake with high bluff banks all around and sinks, and this pool containes quantities of fine fish.

On the west side of the creek makes in a rough rocky ridg and termenates at the creek in a perpendichuler bluff, and thare is the oldest looking Indian signe I ever saw. Pictures of men, women, children, animals, carrecters, and hyrogliphics, in pictures and cut in the bluff. On trees on the east side of the creek is a skirt of various kinds of timber, liveoak, hackberry, elm, and box elder. Callahan hated to be outdone and the Indian trail led straight for this Lost Creek.

The Captain said, "I will leave it to a vote whether we shall go on or turn back."

Thare was twelve voted to go on and eight voted to turn back, the rest not voteing at all.

One man said, "As many as wants to can go on, but if I can git one man to go with me I will turn back."

We was all wanting watter, som real bad, and it was two ha[rd] days march on fresh horses either way, and it was then night and our watter gave out that day at dinner, our horses was tired and som of them lame.

Callahan called Cockrel and myself to him, says he, "Boys, what would you do in a case of this kind."

Cockrel said, "You are the Captain. Do as you think best."

He then looked at me and I says, "Captain, if it was left to me to deside I should turn back for two reasons. One is I dont believe we can overtake the Indians and the other is som of the men and horses is now give out and it will be a hard matter to git home at best."

Next morning after we had mounted Callahan mad us a short speech and said all those that is willing to go on to ride six paces to the front and those who wished to turn back to stand fast. Thare was only six rode out and we all agreede to turn back, but owing to som contraryness som of the men did not want to go back the way we came and wanted to take a diferent route, saying we could reach the Colorado River sooner by takeing a difrent route.

Cockrel said to me, "They will miss it badly, but we can stand it if they can."

So we let them go their way and we traveled on and on. It was a hot day and som of the men already spitting cotton, som cursing and nearly all fretting, and we did not stop for noon that day but went on until night. That was the thirty third night out from Seguin and our grub was all out as well as watter.

Next morning we was in our sadles long long before sunup following out the same corse as they thought that [they was] traveling the day before, but when the sun rose it did not rise in the right place to suit som of us.

Cockrel says to me, "We are within four hours ride of the place whare we turned back yesterday morning."

I says, "Do you think so!"

He says, "Yes, I know it!"

I made it known to the Captain and he called a halt but som of the men was loth to halt but did at the second call, and Callahan told Cockrel to state his belief and reasns which he did in a few words. Som of the men laughed, som cursed, and one old man saud that Cockrel dident know the musle of his gun from a hole in the ground.

Cockrel says, "Well, boys, go ahead if you think thare is no hell or hereafter."

They went and about 10 oclock we reached the mountain, but they did not believe it to be the same mountain until they went round to whare we had dug for watter, and then thare was such a torrent of curses, enough to raise the hair on any Christian mans head, cursing the luck, the world, by sections, then by half inches, and the devil, and God, and everything that they could think of and they thought of a heap.

I tell you shore we stayed thare and rested until about one oclock and started on again, but this time with our guide and myself in front takeing a difrent corse from the one we had trav-

eled the day before. We had been then two days and nights without watter and one day and night without food and our horses
had been four days and nights without watter. The boys was all
gitting in a bad fix especily John R. King. His toung was so swol-
len that he could hardly [close] his mouth and som others nearly
as bad. Myself, Cockrel and Callahan did not seem to suffer like
[the others,] perhaps becase we did not fret like som, and we
rode hard all that day.

Late in the evening I kiled an old poor antelope and we camped
and devoured the thing boddy and soul, and next morning we
was in our saddles early, traveled hard until near one oclock
when we reached the foot of a mountain, high and covered with
scrubby brush, and several ledges of large rough scraggy bould-
ers. Thare was a large grove of live oak trees forming a dence
shade with flowing grass underfoot and it was so inviting, as it
was very hot at that time of day, that King perposed to stop and
rest and graze our horses, and then travel in the night to make up
lost time and we all agreede.

After we had unsaddled and staked our horses, Cockrel perposed to me for us to go up on the mountain and spy out to see
if we could discover any sign of a watter corse ahead of us. We
taken our guns and started up the mountain when Callahan says,
"Boys, try to kill something or come back soon for we must draw
lots to see whoes horse shall be kiled this evening."

He said this in a joke, but it sounded dreadfully like earnest,
and it filled my mind with such awe that it struck a thrill to my
very soul and we went on up the mountain to the first ledg of
rocks which was near half was up the mountain and sat down
to rest.

We rested but a few minutes when Cockrel rose up and said,
"You can sit still and rest. I will go on up to the next ledg."

He crawled, for it was so steepe he coul[d] not walk, up to the
ledg and sat down and I started on and [as] I reached the ledg
he rose and started on, and I went [a few] feete to the right of
whare he had sat and whare [thare wa]s a ledg whare a large
boulder had broken of and fell over and left a space of about two

"And I involenterily prayed"

feet at the bottom between it and the main rock. I sat down on the rock with my feete hanging of in the space between and fell into the following train of thoughts,

"Well, we are gitting in a terable fix, men almost dieing with hunger and thirst and a propersition made to cast lots to see whoes horse shal be kiled for his blood to quinch the thirst of famishing men. Well, I cant think of a paralel in history unless it was the case of Samson of old who slew a thousand Philistians with the jawbone of an ass and after finishing his work he threw down the bone and sat down. He was so tired, so exausted, so thirsty and so hot, he said to himself, for thare was no one near, so now I must die for the want of watter to quinch my thirst, and he prayed to the Lord to send him watter and when he was well nigh in dispair he looked to the jawbone and saw watter gushing out of it and he slacked his thirst and revived.

Then again, Elija prayed for rain after a three years and a half drouth and God sent him rain in answer to his petition." I says "Thare was a God in those days and thare is certainly the same God now and that he is as willing to hear and answer prayr as he was then, and I thought now why cant he show his great compashion to a fiew of the workmanship of his own hands," and I involenterily prayed almost without knowing it, thus,

"Now O God, thou art the same God, thou art Samsons God, thou art Elijas God, and thou are our God, and now, if it is thy will, now make they Great Power manifest in some way that these poor suffering creatures may realize that thou art God!"

[The last part of this chapter is missing from the manuscript. The subtitles in the chapter heading indicate the contents of the lost pages.]

CHAPTER IV

Callahans Minute Men. Burlesons Fight With Cordova. Wounding of Milford Day. Trial and Killing of Prisners. Council House Fight in San Antonio. Andrew Sowell Misses Deer and Long Fire.

❦ IN THE SPRING of 1839 Capt. Callah[an o]rdered the writer, me, to take three men and go up the San Jeronemo and over to Yorks Creek and back down Mill Creek on a scouting mission. I taken Andrew Sowell, John Sowell and James Roberts and went up the San Jeronemo and over to Yorks Creek and camped at a watter hole until we kiled two fat deer a peace and fleaced of the flesh, packed up and started accross to the head of Mill Creek. In order to fill out our time we aimed to strike the river and kill some turkey and go in next day.

Ed Burleson, then liveing on the Colorado River, somhow or other had got wind of Cordovas outfit and hastily geathered togeather about 80 men, and he fell in behind Cordova and was in full chace after him. I had with my scout crossed their course ahead of them, and we assended a ridg and I looked back and to my right and saw a purfect swarm of buzzards all going south.

I says, "Boys, what does that mean," pointing to the large gang of buzzards.

We all stoped and watched them a few seconds. Som said one thing and som a[nother].

Andrew Sowell says, "I will tell you what I th[ink it] means. Thare has been a larg boddy of Indians [on the w]ay down and them buzzards is [following them, and if that] is the case, as we have cros[sed ahead of them we] should go see."[1]

[1] This part of Nichols' manuscript is badly torn and many pieces are missing. A. J. Sowell in *Rangers and Pioneers of Texas* (San Antonio: Shepard Bros. & Co., 1884), p. 186, gives the following account: " 'I will tell you what I think they mean,' said Andrew, after looking at them a short time, 'they are following a large body of Indians or men of some kind, to pick up what is left about the camps. I remember when we were following the Indians the time they killed Greser, and his Mexicans, a raven kept ahead of us all the time, following in the wake of the Indians, and

I says, "Boys, if it is Indians thare may be a larg crowd of them and they are makeing directly for Seg[uin,] and we are heavily sacked and are nearer to Seguin than we are to whare them guns fired. I think [it] would be more prudent for us to hasen to town and not[ify] the people, git she[d] of our heavy packs, git the Captain and som more of the boys, and then go and see what it means."

They all agreede and we started for home.[2] We rode as fast as we could with our heavy packs and when we arived we learned that two of Burlesons men had come in and reported that Burleson had attacted Cordova that evening and had a runing fight and had killed and wounded over half his nomber.[3]

The citizens was in conciderable excitement. This was the 14th of March 1839 and Captain Callahan was makeing preparations

would fly up from their camps at our approach. The Indians kill game along the route of their march, which draws the carrion crows; and they will some times follow the trail for days and weeks.' 'Well, then,' said his companion, 'if that is the case, let's go back to town and give the alarm; likely they are on their way to attack the place.' 'No; I am not satisfied yet, I want to see further,' said Andrew, 'you go back and tell them to be on their guard, and I will see if I can make any further discoveries.' And accordingly they separated, Andrew going across to the head of Mill Creek, and then turning south towards the Guadalupe River."

[2] Nichols' version differs from Sowell's version (see note 1). Nichols wrote from personal experience and Sowell from what he heard from his uncles Andrew and John.

[3] Sowell (*ibid.*, p 187) says: ". . . learned from them that a battle had just been fought there between Burleson's Rangers and a motley crowd of Mexicans, runaway negroes and Bilouxie Indians, under General Cordova."

A monument on U.S. Highway 90, five miles east of Seguin, marks the location of this battleground, which is off the highway some distance to the north. The inscription reads: "BATTLEGROUND PRAIRIE, where 80 volunteers commanded by General Edward Burleson defeated Vicinte Cordova and 75 Mexicans, Indians, and Negroes, March 29, 1839, and drove them from Texas, ending the 'Cordova Rebellion.' 25 of the enemy were killed. Many volunteers were wounded, but none fatally."

Background of the Cordova Rebellion is given by Willie Mae Weinert in *An Authentic History of Guadalupe County* (Seguin, Texas: *Seguin Enterprise*, 1951), p. 55: "The battle is called by Wilbarger, The Cordova Fight; and by A. J. Sowell, Battle Ground Prairie Fight. Cordova with his followers were a part of a plan of the Mexican Government to regain control of Texas. They were ordered to organize the Indians, and such others as was possible, to harass the settlers. The infant town of Seguin appeared to be the object of their attack. But Col. Edward Burleson was in pursuit, and was joined by the 'Minute Men of Seguin' in making the attack that caused Cordova to beat a rapid retreat toward Mexico."

to guard the town, but the alarm was so sudent and it was so late thare was no horses brought in, but we had our horses though tired, and we was put on picket guard.

About midnight I went to one of the boys and said, "Cordova has changed his coarse and they are not comeing here. Lets quit our posts and go in and make preparations to start at daylight and see whare they have gone."

We went in and reported our belief and intention to Callahan. He says, "All right, Jim, git ready [to go] and I will go too."

We made ready for an early start but [about] one hour before day Brother John Nichols cam[e i]n without a[ny bullets] for his gun and reported [killing an Ind]ian [that tri]ed twice to make his escape and that [he did] not [think that] was all kilt for as he started of [he saw ano]ther was shot. I went to John B[ox a]s a good one to [help] bring in the w[ounded and] he said he could help me.

By this time day was breaking and while we was harnessing up the horses Dave Runnels came in and repor[ted] none kilt but that Milford was badly wounded [and] that Tom Nichols was with him. Dave had been hit with a larg ball just below the collarbone, and the ball was burred and was still sticking in his breast with a peace of his shirt under it.

We then started after Milford and found him suffering very mutch. It seems that they was all sleeping soundly and dreaming perhaps of the fat turkies they was going to git in the morning, and after Cordova had been defeated by Burleson, he changed his coarse to a ford on the river near six miles above Seguin whare Milford and his men were camped. Cordova was not aware that any one was near the ford, but som of them being afoot, haveing lost their horses in the fight, and seeing the boys horses staked out mad for them. The horses commenced snorting and awoke Milford just as one of them was untying his horse. Milford supposed that the Indians had followed them in to steal their horses, snatched up his gun and fired at the one that was untying his horse and he fell. That raised the other three boys and the firing became general on both sides and lasted several minuts.

After Milford discharged his gun he was standing on his knees reloading when the ball struck him just back of the hip, go[ing in h]is back and down by his left kidney [and out] his right hip. Brother Thomas fired about then [at the] same man that shot Milford. [Th]are was twenty or thirty of th[em In]dians and Mex[icans] and Milford was afraid they wo[uld find] him and he asked Tom to drag him down the bank into the watter, which he did, and held him thare in the river under the bluff until their enemys left.

As they themselves ware on the run they did not tarry long, as the rangers could hear them when they was crossing the river. They listened to the receding clatter of their horses feete until they ware convinced the enemy had left, and Tom taken his charge and swam down to the ford a distance of two hundred yards, and draged him out on the bank whare we found them. We taken them home but Milford had a lingering hard and pain- ful time before he recovered, and after he was thought to be well his hip rose and several peaces of bone worked out. Then for many years he had to undergo the same pain and suffering from his hip riseing and peaces of slivered bones working out. He finely recovered after years of pain and suffering, but it mad a cripple of him for life, but he is still liveing at this writing and limping around on one short leg and has seen as many ups and downs since that time as any man of his age.[4]

The next morning after the battle Burlesons men, 8 in nomber, brought in three negro prisnrs for the purpose of selling them at auction to the highest bidder. One of the prisnrs was an old gray haired man somthing near sixty years old, another one was a stou[t] likely negro man seemeingly thirty five years of age, the other a stout likely boy of sixteen summers and wounded in several places. They ware crossing the high prairie north east of Seguin when the old negro accosted one of the guards [with], "What you going to do with us."

One of the guards spoke and said, "We [ought] to drown you as we could," in a jokeing way.

---

[4] "One of the settlers, James Day, not yet old enough to own 'his share of Se- guin' in his own name, was one of the Seguin Minute Men so seriously wounded that he became a cripple for life and was one of the earliest Texans to be pensioned by the Republic of Texas," (*ibid.*).

The old negro would not take this for an answer but look[ed] at John Box, who was sargeant of the guarde, as though [he] had put the question to him.

Box said, "I am not aware of what disposition will finely be made of the prisnrs, but I have been informed that it is likely that you will all be sold and the money divided amongst the men that captured you to pay them for their trouble."

The old negro then said, "You had better kill us now, for we will fight till we die before we will be slaves again. Do you see them hills," pointing to the Chapote Hills which stood out in bold relief on the south side of the river twelve miles below Seguin and can be seen from a great distance from almost any direction.

Box says, "Yes."

The negro continued, "When I was a young man I worked in a silver mine with the Mexicans in them hills, and I have been free ever sence, but before I was free I kilt women and children enough to swim in their blood if collected to one place. I kilt my master and his whole family, nine in nomber, to git my freedom, and I wont be a slave long at a time any more."

Col. Burleson had preceded the prisnrs to Seguin and was w[ai]ting their comeing. When Box arived with the prisnrs he informed Burleson of the conversation by the negro. Burleson called Captain Callahan, George W. Nichols,[5] John G. Gray, Paris Smith, French, and Abraham Roberts to sit as a court martial, the prisnrs were brought before this court martial and they interogated the old negro first. He stated the same thing to the court that he had stated to Box with the ad[dit]ion that he would fight til he died before [he would be a slave again to any] master. The court passed sentence [that he] suffer the penelty of death by being shot until dead.

The middle aged negro was then braught forward and int[ero]gated. He said he had never kilt any boddy but would if nessasary to gain his freedom if he was put back in slavery.

"Now," said he, "If you will turn us loose we will go to Mexico and promace to never bother white folks again, but wont be a slave again, we have been free too long."

<hr />

[5] This was George Washington Nichols, the father of James Wilson Nichols.

The court gave him the same sentance and to be executed with the old one. The boy was next braught before the court and interogated. He said he was willing to be sold into slavery again, that he had not been free very long and the first time he ran away he was caught and had to take five hundred lashes on his bareback, and now the second time I ran away I have been shot in four places and captured again, and I am tired of such a life as them colord men, pointeing to the two negroes that had been sentanced, calls freedom. The court sentanced him to be sold as a slave to the highest bidder.

Thare came a runner from Burlesons home stateing to Burleson that a member of his family was dangerously ill. Burleson turned the whole business over to Captain Callahan to obey the mandates of the courtmartial and left for home with a few of his men to accompany him. That night Callahan placed a double guard around the prisnrs and the next day he marched them accross the branch and up the slope west of town about a half mile and halted them under a clump of liveoaks. The two negroes was furnished with tools and mad to dig their [own] graves. The old one worked away [as cal]mly as if he [ware] workeing for wages, but after gitting the [graves] part [dug] the young one relented and commenced to beg for his life, but Callahan said sentance had been passed on him by higher authority and he would do his duty. The negro resumed his labors with teares in his eyes but all to no purpose.

When the graves was finished Callahan ordered 8 of his men to take 8 of Burlesons mens guns and step of behind som brush and load four of them with powder and ball, the other four with powder and paper wads. They did so and braught them back and leaned them against one of the trees and Callahan then ordered 8 of Burlesons men to march passed the tree and each one to take a gun. The negroes was then mad to kneel on the brink of the grave and Callahan then blindfolded them himself, placed the men and gave orders to fire, and both negroes rolled of into the grave. After the grave was filled up they proceded to sell the boy who had been marched thare for the double purpose of witnessing the execution of his comrads and being sold. John

B. Gray cried the sale, the bidding was lively for a while but soon thare was but two bidders. Finely he was knocked of to Henry Peck for 451 dollars. One writer I have noticed writeing on this subject says the boy sold for 800 dollars but my journal says 451.[6] This place is within thirty steps of General Jeffersons yard gate whare his residence now stands.

This man Peck who purchest the negro boy was a yankey from Ioway.[7] He had purchased a peace of land at and about the mouth of Mill Creek and cut a race accross the bend of the river and built a griss mill and said he needed [a young] boy to he[lp hi]m. He gave the boy good attention and Peck said he was a good study hand and seemingly well satisfide.

The next summer after Peck had owned him near a year thare was a croud of boys and men in bathing in a long deepe pool just below the mill. The pool was near two hundred yards long and, about forty yards below whare they ware bathing, the river mad a sharpe turn round a point of brush. The negro boy finding a few minuts laisure from his labors, came down allso to bathe and after divesting himself of his apperial he took a runing start and plunged in head first and went under out of sight. He was a good swimmer and a good diver but he was never seen after that leap into the watter.

Thare was som conjectures that he swam under watter until he arived round the bend then rose and mad his escape. My belief is that an alagaitor caught him for thare was a great many alagaitors in the river at that point and som very large ones, and, now, had it not been for the wounding of Day and the graves of the two negroes, all traces of Burlesons fight with Cordova might long sence been obliterated and forgotten, but thare is always somthing to keepe such heroic deeds green in memory.

It was now near the time for the treaty with the Comanche Indians at San Antonio whare they was to meete and smoke the pipe of peace with the whites, so John Sowell and myself con-

[6] The writer referred to was A. J. Sowell (*Rangers and Pioneers of Texas*, p. 188).

[7] The Territory of Iowa, created July 4, 1838, included the present states of Iowa, Minnesota, and parts of North and South Dakota east of the Missouri River. See Cochran and Andrews, *Concise Dictionary of American History*, p. 491.

cluded to go and see what was to be seen. The treaty was to take place March the 19th, 1940. The Indians had already arived and pitched their tents on the Almos[8] three miles from town, but the town was litterly alive with Indians. The comissioners was thare and the government had taken the precaution to send Captain Howard with 30 well armed men as guards.

The day came and with it came ten of the most promanent chiefs and 38 wariors all well armed, thare was ten comissioners to balance against the ten chiefs. They set Captain Howard to watch the 38 wariors and the Council chose a [central] house,[9] a strong one storry house with no windows, and as they entered the [house they ware] disarmed. The redskins did not like this mutch but they all entered. It was observed that the Indians had not braught in the white prisnrs, and suspecting thare would be a row about it, Captain Redd of San Antonio organized all the loose men in town into a company to be ready if anything should happen, and John Sowell and myself joined him.

The Indians had braught in a negro boy and a Mexican man who had been with them twelve years and who was their interpeter. After they was all seated the first question asked was whare are the white prisnrs that you promaced to bring in to this talk. The Mexican, after consulting the head chief, said, "We braught in all the prisnrs we had in our possession, the others are with a roveing band that is not willing to treat."

The whites commenced going out one at a time until all but four was out. The head chief says in broaken Inglish, "Well, how you likee." The whites shook their heads and two more went out, and the chief says, "Well what you doee." The other two mad for the door and at the door they told the interpeter to tell them they would all be held as prisnrs of war until the white prisnrs was braught in, then they shut the door and bared it.

As soon as the interpeter told them their fate they raised the war hoop and the 38 outside mad a rush for the door to free their

---

[8] Olmos Creek, in San Antonio.

[9] The location of the Council House was on Main Plaza in San Antonio. See Edward W. Heusinger, *A Chronology of Events in San Antonio* (San Antonio: Privately published, 1951).

chiefs but narry one reached it. They strung their bows and raised the war hoop, but outside Captain Redd and Howard with their companies was ready and the fight opened. The chiefs burs down the door and rushed out but was shot down as fast as they come out and the fight became general and lasted about a half hour. Altho the Indians faught despretly, we taken one old squaw and our loss was one man, Bill Henson, kilt and seven wounded.[10]

They taken the old squaw and told her if she told them a lie they would kill her but if she would tell them the truth they would turn her loose, then asked her whare the white prisnrs was. She said one they kilt, one they sold to another tribe, and thare was five at camp, was all they had taken that she knew of. She said she was the wife of the head chief Buffalo Hump who had just been kilt and that she was now in full command until another head chief was elected, and if we would go with her to the camp she would deliver the prisnrs to us.

We taken her to camp and found five of the captives. One young girl, Fanny Putnam, had been sold and one of the young ladies, Rhoda Putman, had been taken by a young chief for a wife and had a child by him and would not leave her chief and child to come in, and the youngest Lockhart child they kilt the first day for crying. We taken the other young lady Matilda Lockhart and her sister, the two youngest Putman girls, and the boy Jim Putman, and when he became a man he married one of my sisters.

Fanny Putman, that was sold to another tribe, was afterwards purchesed in Masouri and som twenty years afterwards braught to Gonzales and was recognized by her parance, and the other one died with the Indians. The Comanches was so completely beaten and out done they hung around San Antonio for several months brooding over their lost ten chiefs. They finely bundled up and went high up on the watters of the Colorado River whare we shall leave them.

[10] Nichols is mistaken about the number killed and wounded. In both the *Memoirs of Mary Maverick* (San Antonio: Alamo Printing Co., 1921) and John Henry Brown's *Indian Wars and Pioneers of Texas* (Austin: L. E. Daniell, 1896) the numbers given are seven killed and eight wounded.

Now the life and doings of Andrew J. Sowell is already out and I shal not say mutch for or against him. One incident will sufise though he was my step brother, my father haveing married his mother in 1839. But to the incident. A croud of us was out on a camp hunt this same fall. We found several bee trees and filled all of our vessels and had som ten or fifteen gallons more than we had vessels to hold it, and it was sugested that we kill a deer and cure the hide to carry the honey home in. As Andrew and myself was concidered the most succesfull hunters we was to try our luck first, so we mounted our horses and set out on our mission and we hunted until late that evening when we ware rideing slowly and I was in front and discovered an old bucks head and hornes over a log.

I says, "Be still. Theres a deers head."

It was about one hundred yards away, and I was about dismounting when Andrew says, "Let me shoot. Not that I think I am a better shot than you, but my gun is larger in the bore than yours and is more apt to kill if it hits."

I says, "I believe I can hit his head from here."

Andrew says, "No, dont risk it. I can git to yon tree and then I can hit his eye."

The tree was over half way to the deer. I says, "Try it."

Then he slid of his horse and commenced crawling. The deer had not discovered us. Andrew went half bent to the tree, and then peeped first on one side and then on the other, and then lay down flat on the ground and commenced slideing himself along until I became almost out of patiance, but after so long a time he arived at a saplin not over thirty steps from the deer, and he raised his gun by the side of the saplin and fired.

When the gun fired I, being on horseback, could see the deers head fall to the ground, but at the nois of the gun another buck with head and hornes jumped to his feete and away he ran with his tail up.

I taken Andrews horse by the bridle and led him up to whare Andrew was. He was cursing and beating his old gun with his fist and about the time I got to him he drew his hacknife and commenced to hack his gun stock to peaces. He beat his gun withe his knuckles and hand until his hand was so swolen next day he could use them with great difficulty.

I says, "Whats the matter. Are you crazy."

He says, "No, but this old gun is. Why, if she had not mad long fire I could have hit that deers eye."

I says, "May be you did."

He says, "Hit. Hell. Dident you see him run of untouched."

I says, "Well you kilt one anyhow."

He says, "Its you thats crazy. I seed the deer git [up] and run of."

I says, "Well, you kilt one anyhow."

He says, "I didenot."

I says, "You did."

He says, "I dident for by the Lord, I had taken my gun down when she fired and I know I missed it ten feete."

I says, "You kilt one anyhow."

He says, "You are a fool. Dident I see the deer [git] up and run of."

I saw his nose begin to swell and [I] knew he was gitting mad. I says, "Andrew, you kilt a deer, and if you will go to the log you will see."

He was so confident that thare was but one buck, and he saw him git up and run of, that he would not go only about thirty steps to see. By this time he had quit hacking his gun and commenced reloading, and wh[en] he finished and steped towards his horse I says, "Lets g[o] skin the old buck."

He says, "By the Lord, dont say bu[ck] to me again."

I knew then he was gitting hot so I sayed no more, and he mounted his horse and galloped of in the direction the well deer had went. I stood gazeing after him until he was out of sight then led my horse to the log and examined the old buck. The ball had taken effect in his head and the brains was oozeing out at the bullet hole. The sun was now nearly down and I was near two miles from camp, so I lifted him into my saddle and mounted up behind and set out for camp. On ariveing I found that Andrew had not yet put in an apearence and I told the story to the other boys and they laughed harty.

As soon as Andrew arived they commenced to tease him. They would go up to him and look at his swolen fist and say, "Long fire," then look at the hacks on his gun and say laughing, "Long fire," until he became fighting mad. Then they would hush awhile. After that if any of us said, "Long Fire," we had simpley to git out of Andrews way.

CHAPTER V

---

*On A Hunt. Almost Run Over By Herd Of Buffalo. Attacted
By Wolves. Death Of James Campbell. Takeing A Load Of
Pecans to Port Lavaca. Almost Freezing to Death. Indian
Outrages.*

AFTER THIS the writer was compairitively idle the rest of
this fall and winter except for hunting. One time we was out and
kilt a fine lot of fat turkies and taken a large fat bear in out of the
wet. We then mooved over to Plumb Creek whare Lockhart now
stands and finished killing as many turkies as we wanted. In a
few days we then mooved up to the head of that creek to kill som
more deer and we camped at a watterhole several days and kilt a
fine lot of deer, and we now concluded to strike out for Austin and
finish out the load, as we traveled.

One morning the hunters scattered out over the prairie and I
was driveing leisurely along when all at once I heared a tremen-
dious roaring like a terriable storm comeing up. I turned my head
and saw several thousand buffaloes comeing directly behind me,
and, knowing that hardly anything would turn a large herd of
buffalo when excited and runing, I could not see neither edge of
them nor the hindmost end of the herd.

The hunters had given them a scare and they ware runing
from them. I saw my danger at a glance and stoped my team,
jumped out and hobbled my lead steer, but by this time they ware
in less than one hundred yards of the wagon and the breast of
the mooveing mass seemed to be at least a mile wide and me
about the center, and I had not time for any other preparations.

I jumped in the wagon and snatched up my rifle, and about the
time the wagon was in danger of being run over I fired and the
re[por]t of the gun parted the hurd in front. I whooped and
ho[llere]d and mad such a nois dischargeing my side [arm
while] waveing a red blanket, the whole hurd parted at the hind-
end of my wagon but closeing in again just ahead of my oxen,

passing in three or four feete of the wagon, and my oxen reared and plunged but could do nothing els.

After the liveing current had subsided I looked and saw a dead buffalo lying about thirty yards distant ahead of me. My shot had taken effect and I left my wagon and teem standing and went to examin it and found it to be a nice fat three year old cow, and I went back, drove up close to her, hobbled out my oxen, and commenced to skin her.

The hunters commenced comeing in one or two at a time until all had arrived, each one congratulating me on my narrow escape and good luck in killing such a fine buffalo. They had seen the hurd and gave chase but fell fare behind. We sent of for a keg of watter and camped thare that night, and cut out such peaces as we wanted to carry to market that night and left the carkes on the ground.

After cooking and eateing to our harts content we spread our blankets and prepared to take som rest, but thare seemed to be no rest for the wicked day nor night, for we had not been still but a few minutes when a gang of wolves set up such a continuous howling that we could not sleepe, and it seemed the wolves for miles around had cented the blood and broiling beef and was geath[er]ing togeather for the purpose of makeing a general raid on us. As they advanced they seemed to increase in nombers which was the case, and they would advance a few yards and stop and set up such a turrable houl that rend the air.

Ha[rdin] says, "Boys, we had better git up and give them fellows a little pill or two or we will not git a snooze this night."

We all got up, made a big light with dry mesquit wood, taken our guns, and stood back in the dark so when they came up in the light we could see how to shoot them. We taken a position in a row, and in a few minuts here came twenty five or thirty wolves leaping and growling as they came, and when they got fairly in the light we all fired killing som and wounding others. They retreated a short distance and the wounded ones set up such a houl, or squall and yell, it mad the others mad and they mad a charge on the wounded ones and soon dispatched them and silenced the fuss, then set up a long mournful lonesom houl for about five minuts seemeingly to call all their reinforsements in to line.

By this time we ware all reloaded, and they now mad a furious charge on us right up to the fire and while in the light, we all fired with about the same result as before, but this time they did not retreat after their wounded but charged right on through the fire light and over the carkes of the buffalo.

We all taken to the wagon for refuge and stood in the wagon and shot all of our fire arms emty then drew our hack knives and fought them of from climbing into the wagon, cutting of their feete and hacking their noses, and while som of them keept us treed in the wagon, others ware helping themselves on the carkes.

They keept us in the wagon near a half hour, and while som of us ware keeping them at bay, others ware loading and shooting as fast as they could, nor did they retreat until they had cleaned all the meat of the bones of the buffalo, and they retreated in good order of about fifty yards and set up a houl of defiance and disapeared, leaving more than twenty dead on the ground and as many badly wounded.

Our loss was slight, only a potion of courage missing. We could not count them in the dark but they was variously estemated by us at from fifty to five hundred, and the next morning we dispached the wounde[d] close by, hitched up, and roled out for Austin.

We found Congress in session in a double log cabin about sixty feete square with back rooms on north side which served as commity rooms.[1] We sold out our load for a good price and returned and kilt a fine load of meat to take home.

And now, dear reader, if it is posable for you to doubt this snake story about the wolves, you can go and examen the battleground for yourselves, for I assure you the men that partisipated in that afair is all dead and gone whare the woodbine twineth and the wangdoodle mourneth for her first born, and I only am

---

[1] "The Temporary Capitol for the use of Congress was built on Lots 9, 10, and 11, in Block 98. . . . It fronted to the east and was but one story high. A broad hall extended east and west, behind which were committee rooms. The Senate Chamber was in the north end and the Hall of the House in the South" (Alex W. Terrell, "The City of Austin from 1839 to 1865," *Quarterly of the Texas State Historical Association*, XIV, No. 2 [October, 1910], p. 119).

left alone with my journal or memorandom book to tell the story.

After we returned from Austin all was quiet around Seguin except ocaisional raid by the Waco Indians, as we could always tell when that tribe sent in a thieveing party as the Bigfoot Waco, as we always called him, was shore to be in the croud, and continual raiding was kept up in and around San Antonio by the Waco and Tawackane tribes.

A few days after my return James Campbell came to me and said he had som business in San Antonio that he was oblige to tend to himself, and the Indians was so bad out thare that he wanted five or six men to go with him as a guard. He said he would give a dollar a day and foot all the bills.

"Now," said he, "If you will go git up a croud to suit yourself and here take that for your trouble," handing me a five dollar gold peace. "I want to start tomorrow at ten oclock."

I went round and got Brother Solomon, Jim Roberts, John Sowell, and Hardin Turner, and between sundown and dark we arived at the ditch in the edg of town, when Campbell purposed to turn down the ditch and camp as thare was good grass and watter. We struck camp and turned our horses loose to graze until after supper, then tied them up for the night, and about one hour before day next morning we all turned [them] loose again, and after breakfast we all started after our horses and all found our horses but Campbell. He kept scircleing farther and farther from camp, and by this time the rest of us was all saddled and was going to help hunt the missing horse but just then we heard Campbell hollow and we suposed he had found his horse and hollowed to let us know that he had found him, so we would not go to help hunt.

We waited and waited, he did not come so about sunrise we all mounted and went in the direction we had heard him hollow, but we had no suspitions of Indians until we rode upon his boddy, and he had been kilt, skelped, and striped.[2] We taken the trail and they put me ahead to trail.

[2] Sowell (*Rangers and Pioneers*, p. 202) tells the story: ". . . they came across two little Mexican boys who were making their way to town as fast as they could run, and seemed greatly frightened and nearly out of breath. They said . . . the

I says, "Boys, if you will keep up with me we will catch th[e] redskins."

They all said, "Light out."

I struck a gallope and run the trail about seven miles on the divide between the Almos and Salow[3] when we came in sight of two Indians and quickened our pace, and Brother Solomon and I soon distanced the other boys and we ran side by side, neither one of our horses could gain on the other.

One of the savages found we was going to out run him and he threw himself of his horse and prepared to fight. He strung his bow and was adjusting an arrow when we both fired at the same time, both balls takeing effect in his brea[s]t, cutting his bow string and shivering his bow in splinters, and the redskin bit the ground.

We knew it was no use to give chase to the other redskin for he was on Campbells horse, the best horse in the croud, and he mad good his escape. So we taken the dead savages horse and accuterements and returned and burried Campbell, but the savage that got away must have had Campbells cloths containing his money and papers as they was never recovered.

After returning to Seguin, in a few days the citizens mad up money to buy a load of corn for bread and hired me to haul it. On my way down I met Alsa Miller on his way up to Seguin to hire me to drive a team to Port Lavaca loaded with pecans. We agreede, and he turned back, and I went on to Col. King whare I expected to buy the corn, and while thare I told Col. King that I had hired to Miller to drive his team.

King was auful mad, cursed Miller and said, "I hired Miller to ride to Seguin and hire you to drive my team and now the rascal has hired you to drive his team." Said he, "Dam him, Ill git eaven with him for it."

Indians ran a man down the hill and caught up with him near where they hid. They said he was a big man with long arms, and having nothing to shoot with, stopped at a pile of rocks, and fought the Indians with them as long as he could stand up, but being shot full of arrows, he finally sunk down and the Indians went to him. . . . The rangers knew the man was Jim Campbell . . . they found Campbell horribly mutilated and scalped and with a curse on the bloody fiends the rangers bore their dead comrade back to camp."

[3] Olmos and Salado creeks, near San Antonio.

I got the corn, and he told me to hire him a driver if I could, and I went back to Seguin and hired Hardin Turner for King and we went down.

King had a large heavy wagon with 103 bushels of pecans loose in the bed and five big fat yoake of oxen to draw it. Miller had a truck wagon, the wheeles sawed of a large sicamore log, with 106 bushels of pecans loose in the bed and seven yoake of steers, all wild but three steers, one gentle yoake for the tongue and one good lead. The others had never been yoaked or hitched.

He said to me, "That is my outfit. Do you think you can manage such a fixup."

I says, "If any boddy can I can."

He says, "I knew that and I also knew that you could have done better with the old Col. but I knew I could not git another man to take the job, and now King wont give but six bits a day. If you will go, I will go with you and help you all I can and give you a dollar a day from the time you left home until you git back home."

King sent his son, young John, to help Turner and we all got ready and started the 7th day of December calculating to make the round trip by Christmas, and we had no mishaps until we reached the nine mile point above Victory.[4] It was a warm sultry evening, every leaf was at rest and we could hear not a sound save the harp of a thousand strings which the musketoes played round our ears. It was between sundown and dark, so we drove to the highest place on the point in order to catch the breeze, if any, and to leave all the musketoes we could in the valley below.

After supper we crawled in our wagons and lay down on the naked pecans to keep cool. We lay thare and faned musketoes with our hats until, about ten oclock, thare blewup a brisk norther with a heavy mist of rain with it, and we soon got cool enough and the musketoes was no whare to be found, but the wind increased and the rain fell fast so that in two hours every thing exposed was covered with ice and sleete.

We tryed every plan to keepe warm but we had no wood and

[4] This is the town of Victoria, on the Guadalupe River about twenty-five miles from Port Lavaca.

if we had the wind blew so hard we could not have kept a fire.
Miller and myself got so cold we got up and commenced walking
to try to keepe warm but in vain, and we ran round and cut the
hobbles of all the oxen so they could go to the river bottom. We
walked and troted and stamped around to keepe our joints lim-
ber, we knew we would not freeze as long as we keept mooveing
but in the wind we could not keepe warm.

I says to Miller, "Them boys will freeze to death if they lay
thare if they are not already dead."

Miller says, "Lets go see," and we went to the wagon and
called them.

We whooped and hollowed and got no answer, and Miller
geathered one of them by the feete and draged him to the front
end of the wagon and I the[n] taken the other, and we draged
them out and rubed and pounded them so they parcially came
too so they could stand on their feete.

Turner walked a few steps by holding to the wagon but King
refused to step and Miller got the oxwhip and come down on him
like he was killing snakes, telling him he would whip him to
death if he did not walk, so King steped round a little but they
was both so cold their legs was stiff.

Miller said that King and Turner would both freeze to death if
thare was not somthing done and done quick, and he told me to
drive them round til he got his horse and he would take them one
at a time to the river bottom a half mile away. I tried to drive
them but they would not drive worth a cent for me, so when Miller returned with his horse King could not or would not moove a
peg. We raped som blankets round him, put him up behind, tied
him on like a bag of meal and Miller mounted and away they
went, and as luck would have it, they found som freighters thare
with a larg fire, but King was so nigh dead that Miller had to
stay thare and work with him to bring him too.

By this time the rain had sceased but the wind stil blew a perfect harican and the ground, grass, bushes, and evrithing was
covered several inches in sleete and ice. Miller stayed so long I
began to git uneasy for fear King had fell of and Miller could not
git him up again, and I told Turner that I could stand it no longer

and if he would pick up couriage and start I knew he could go and if anything had happened to the boys we would find them on the way and that I was not going to stay thare and freeze to death on his account. He said rather than stay and freeze by himself he would make an effort, so we raped all the bed clothes we could carry round us and started.

At the foot of the ridg thare was a clair runing creek about ten feete wide and about half thigh deepe and we could see the smoke or steam riseing from the watter. Turner said he never would go through that watter for he knew if he got his feete wet he was gone shore, but I told him he could stay thare and freeze, I was going to the bottom, and plunged in and it was as warm as dish-watter so I perswaided him into it and then I could hardly git him out it felt so good, and when I did we went on to the bottom, found the fire and Miller stil rubing and working with King, and I am satisfied that warm watter seaved mine and Turners feete from frost bite.

King was frostbit from his hips down and his hands from his elbows to the ends of his fingers, and both of Millers hands and feete was mor or less frostbit, and Turners hands was both badly frostbit, and one of mine slightly, but our feete and legs was all right. We stayed thare four or five days until the spell was over and that [was] the bigest sleete I ever saw before or since. We went on and sold out and after takeing Christmas in Victory with Brother John and Bill Harges, who had been caught in the cold snap, we returned.

And now if any of my readers is doubtful as to the truth of this cold story and wants the papers on it, they will only have to go and see or write to John King who is still liveing at this writing, as I saw and talked with him a short time ago. He resides in Live-oak County 25 miles north of Oakeville on the San Antonio and Oakeville Road and keps a dry goods store, and he will cheerfully answer all questions on the subject.

After returning home the writer passed the balance of the winter and early spring in compairetive idleness, nothing tran-spireing of any note. This year of 1840 was notable for incidence in Indian outrages and Indian warfare, but it was mostly in the

"In danger of being run over"

eastern and middle potion of Texas, as the Mexican Government
was continuely sending mesingers amongst the Indians inciteing
them to ware against the whites by fair promaces, until nearly all
the border tribes ware on the the warepath.

On one occaision Lieutenant James O. Rice with a few followers overtaken and defeated one of those agents, Manuel
Flores, and about twenty five followers about fifteen miles south
of Austin near whare the old San Antonio and Nacogdoches Road
crosses Plum Creek.⁵ Flores was killed in this fight with several of
his followers, and Rice lost none kilt and but three wounded, two
slightly and one severly, and Rice captured in this afair 300
pounds of powder, a like quantity of shot balls and barlead, with
45 stand of arms and more than one hundred head of horses and
mules.

On the person of Flores was found letters and papers showing
the grand stratagy of the Mexican policy of inciteing the border
tribes to aid them in their ware with Texas. His instructions was
to the chiefs of the Cadoes, Semenoles, Beloxes, Cherokees, Kicka-
poos, and Comanches promaceing them the lands on which they
had settled and ashureing them they neede expect nothing from
thoes greedy whites, who wished not only to deprive them of
their lands but would deprive the Indian, if posable, of the sun
that warms and vivafies him, and by concert of action at the same
time that the Mexican army marched into San Antonio, the Indians was to light up the whole fronteer with flames of Texas
dwellings and cause the very air to resound with cries of their
women and children.

Our border was in a constant commotion but other writers of
Texas History detailed the war with the Cherokees and other
tribes by the every ready, willing and efficient leader, commander, and fighter, Col. Ed. Burleson, and others farth[er] east
so that I will not attemt it.

⁵ This battle was fought May 15–17, 1839. Brown, in his *Indian Wars and
Pioneers*, p. 65, locates the battle on Brushy Creek below Austin. H. Yoakum, in
his *History of Texas* (2 vols., New York: J. S. Redfield, 1855), II, 260, locates it on
the San Gabriel Fork of Little River. J. W. Wilbarger, in his *Indian Depredations
in Texas* (Austin: Hutchings Printing House, 1889), pp. 157–167, also locates it on
the San Gabriel Fork of Little River.

CHAPTER VI

Indians Raid Linnville. Battle of Plum Creek. Wounded.
Distribution of Spoils of Battle. Errors of Other Writers.

◆ THE COMANCHES [had failed] to accomplish a treaty and being so thor[oughl]y defeated at San Antonio they hung around awhile brooding over their lost ten chiefs, and [later] in the spring of this year 1840, they bundled up and went high up on the watters of the Cololorado and got togeather the whole tribe and thare in council resolved to redress their wrongs received at San Antonio. They elected a head chief and all the subordinent chiefs and layed their plans to over run Texas, and tried to perswaid all the other tribes to assist them and devide the teritory amgst themselves and have big hunting ground, but none of the other tribes would venture to assist them as they could still smell the patching from the campaign of Burleson, Moor, Rusk and others.

They concluded to try a lone hand, but did not even make a point as they got badly enjured. They mad all preperations nessarry for a campain, the grand expedition to Linville, about 1800 wariors all well mounted and armed with six or seven hundred head of loose horses and fat mules for beef with 20 chiefs and 180 boys, women and children. This information I learned from a squaw that was taken prisnr at the battle of Plum Creek.

They emerged from the mountains into the prairie near the Manchac Springs in Hays County, continueing their way down the country between Peach Creek and McLure Hill in Gonzales County, and on down to Victory,[1] which was the first settlement they struck. After killing one man, his wife and two children, and a negro man, his wife and one child, and capturing a negro girl, all at one house in the surburbs of the t[own], they then attacted the town. It was so unexpected that they was wholy unprepard and frightened out of th[eir wi]ts so that they ran into their houses and shut their doors, but seeing the savages prepareing to

---

[1] Victoria, Victoria County.

fire the town, they sallyed out with such arms as the emergency
of the case would permit, about sixty men and drove them from
the town with a loss of nine killed, including one chief, and several wounded, but the citizens had three men wounded. They
drew of about a mile from town and camped and burried their
dead which they carried of the field.

Early next morning the savages renewed the attact on the
town, but it is said experiance teaches knowledg and that nessity
is the mother of invention, and during the night the citizens had
come to their sences and, comprehending their danger they
forted up all the women and children in a larg stone house. The
men got togeather and organized by electing John Polen, an old
Texas vetren, who stil survives and resides near Lagarter,[2] Live
Oak County, and from whom I received my information a short
time after this affair occured, and he was elected leader.

After posting out guards the citizens worked all night in col-
lecting arms, amunition, and preparing to defend the town so
when the attact was made just at daybreak the whites received
them with such a shower of bullets that it mad the savages beat
a hasty retreat, with considerable loss though succeeded in fireing several houses which had been abandoned the night before.
Seeing the citizens of the town was prapared and willing to give
them battle, they did not renew the attact, but after burrying
their dead, which was thought to be about seventeen, they struck
of.

About a mile from to[wn] lived a Mr. Crosby who had been
with his family [on a trip] and knew nothing of the Indians being in the coun[ty. He] had just returned and was in the act of
unharnesing his team when the savages serounded the house and
closed in upon them. They kilt and scelped Crosby and taken
Mrs. Crosby and two small children captive, and, she said, after
outrageing her person, they tied her on a packmule and handed
her her baby and tied her other child on behind her and struck of
in the direction of Linville.[3]

---

[2] Lagarto, Live Oak County.

[3] Sowell (*Rangers and Pioneers*, p. 204) tells it: "The Indians passed through
what is now Caldwell County, which was not organized until eight years after-
ward, and reached Victoria on the 6th of August, and after burning part of the

That evening while crossing the Cassa Blanco Creek they drove the mule on which she rode under som low limbs and hurt her baby so bad that it cryed very loud, and one of these fiends, an old crooked mouthed savage, snatched it from her arms and bursted its braines out against a tree and threw it from him. The mother saw it all but said nothing, only ejeckulated "its better of," and the old savage rode on as composedly as if nothing had happened. That evening near sundown, her little boy began to git tired and thirsty and began crying for watter, and she told him they would kill him if he did not hush, but he only cryed louder. The same old venerable father of the forest drew his knife, cut the straps that bound him to his mother, sliped him of the mule, ran his speer through him, pining him to the ground for a second, then withdrew the reeking speer and left the little fellow for the vultures or wolves to finish. The mother involentaryly screamed and the old savage shook his speer at her as mutch as to say, "Dry up or Ill serve you the same way."

They traveled all night and the next day about 10 oclock, the 8th day of August, they charged into the town of Linville. The citizens took refuge in a small sailboat that stood moored at the landing and escaped. [Mr. Watts,] then collector of costoms at that place, and wife [who] went [back] to secure som valuable papers, money, and jewlrey was left behind, but arived at the watters edg as the boat left the shore and started to wade to the boat, was so hard presed by the savages that Watts was overtaken, kilt, and scelped, and Mrs. Watts captured.

---

town and committing other depredations . . ."

The following account appears in Brown, *Indian Wars and Pioneers*, pp. 79–80: "On the same afternoon [August 6, 1840] the Indians approached Victoria. At Spring Creek above the town, they killed four negroes belonging to Mr. Poages. On the Texana road, east side of town, they met and killed Col. Pinkney Caldwell, a prominent citizen and soldier of 1836. They chased various persons into the town, killing an unknown German, a Mexican, and three more negroes. A party hastily repaired to the suburbs to confront the enemy. Of their number, Dr. Gray, Varlan Richardson, William McNuner and Mr. Daniels were killed, a total of thirteen. The Indians retired and passed the night on Spring creek, having secured about fifteen hundred horses and mules on the prairie in front of Victoria. . . . On Friday, August 7, the Indians reappeared, made serious demonstrations, but were held in check by citizens under cover of houses. Securing several hundred more horses they bore down the country to Nine Mile Point, where they captured young Mrs. Crosby."

The savages then proceded to pillage and rob the town and packed all the goods in packs. After they had ransacked every house they then fired the town, and, as they thought they had overrun Texas and burned the capital, they was ready to return, and they packed all the goods on packmules and started to return.[4]

The next day a company from Quero[5] and Victory hastely geathered came up with them and had several scirmishes with them but was too weeke for a general ingagement. The Indians nessaraly traveled slow so the whites kept close after them annoying them all they could, occaisionly causing one to bite the dust.

The whites sent men ahead every day to recrute and keepe the settlers advised of their whareabouts, and men was sent in every direction whare it was likely men could be found, some to the settlements on the Colorado, C. C. Colley was sent to Gonzales and vecinity to recrute, Ben McCulloch was sent to the settlements above and on to Seguin, all with instructions to rendesvouse at Isham J. Goods ranch which was located on the road leading from Gonzales to Austin and in which direction the savages seemed to be traveling. Goods ranch was six miles east of

[4] Sowell (*Rangers and Pioneers*, p. 205): ". . . went on to Linnville, a trading point on the Lavaca bay, and reached that place on the 8th. Most of the men of the village were absent and the savages proceeded to pillage and burn the place. Three families took refuge on a small sail vessel in the harbor. While Major Watts, collector of customs, was trying to reach the vessel, he was shot down and his wife taken prisoner. From Linnville the Indians hastily withdrew with their valuable booty."

Brown (*Indian Wars and Pioneers*, p. 80: ". . . before dawn on Sunday, August 8 . . . they killed Mr. O'Neal and two negro men belonging to Mr. H. O. Watts. The people, believing the enemy to be friendly Mexicans with horses to sell, realized the fearful truth only in time to escape into the sailboats anchored in shoal water about about one hundred yards from shore. In attempting this, Maj. Watts was killed in the water. His young bride, negro woman, and a little son of the latter were captured. There was an immense amount of goods in the warehouses destined for San Antonio and the Mexican trade. Rapidly were these goods packed on horses and mules but it consumed the day, and late in the afternoon every building but one warehouse was burned, the citizens, becalmed all day in their boats, witnessing the destruction of their homes and business houses."

[5] Cuero, De Witt County.

whare Lockhart now stands. Ben McCulloch t[urned] back from Seguin to make his report to Caldwe[ll who was] then acting as captain of the militia. Thare was a [group of] men started from Seguin and about fifty with Caldwell from Gonzales. We from Seguin arived at the ranch about midnight, about an hour after Caldwell arived with his force near one oclock,[6] and James Byrd came in with a small squad about two hours before day.

Henry McCulloch, who with two or three men had been watching the manuvers of the enemy, came in and reported that the Indians was crossing Plum Creek at that very minute. Caldwell called the men togeather and mad a short speech saying, "If the Indians was not attacted before they reached the mountains, that a thousand men could do nothing with them, that they must be attacted and whiped before they reach the mountains and if they was let alone until twelve oclock that day thare would be no use in following them any farther." And says he, "We have a few over a hundred men and if we cant whipum we can try."

The men all hollowed out, "Hurrah for Caldwell," and we voted him the command, then he said, "Let us be up and doing."

He gave orders to be in our saddles in five minuts, but just before all was mounted thare come a runner from Burleson stateing that that officer would be thare by nine or ten oclock, that Gen'l Felix Houston[7] was with Burleson, and that John H. Moore and Z. N. Morrel was on their way with a goodly nomber of men but could not tell when they would arive. Caldwell sent a runner back to Burleson to double quick or he would be to late as he in-

---

[6] The following account is given in Life of Robert Hall, by "Brazos" (Austin: Ben C. Jones & Company, 1898), p. 49: "We got the news at Gonzales that a strong column of Comanches had passed into the lower country, and we at once got into the saddle and marched to the rescue of our friends. We camped at Isham Good's first, and not hearing any news, we were about to return home when Ben McCulloch rode into camp. Goat Jones was with him. They reported that the Indians had plundered the lower country, and were returning on the same trail."

[7] This is General Felix Huston. His name was often misspelled by Texans of that time, for they all knew Sam Houston and many thought the generals' names were spelled alike. Felix Huston had been made a major general of the Texan Army in 1839 and was in command of the militia. See Brown, Indian Wars and Pioneers, p. 81.

tended to ingague the enemy with what men he had [as] soon as
he should ovetake them.

Caldwell says, "We cant aford to wait for Burleson nor no
other m[an.] I[t is] expediant that the enemy should be attacted
and delayed, if not whiped, before they reach the mountains, for
then all the men in the country could do no good."

There was at least sixty or eighty men hollowed out, "Lead, we
will follow."

Some said, "Catchum Captain."

We mounted just as the bonny gray eyed morning began to
peepe, and marched over the ground whare the town of Lockhart
now stands, and as soon as we reached the prarie Caldwell formed
us in a colum four deepe, and in forming the colum I was thrown
in frunt of one line. In a few minuts we hove in sight of the
enemy and marched on in this posision, the whole colum mooove-
ing on end formost, until we arived within three hundred yards
of the enemy.

As soon as the Indians discovered us they formed in line of
battle but still marched on to a point of timber and halted and
comenced blowing their whistles and howling their war song.
We was ordered to halt still in the same posision, and this halt
was caused by Burleson's command comeing in sight on our
right, and at the same time Burleson and Houston comeing up to
Caldwell in a full run.

Burleson says to Caldwell, "Captain, I thought it nothing but
right for us to tender the command to Genl. Houston as he ranks
us so we wish to know your mind on the subject."

Caldwell says, "Of corse, he is intitled to the command as he
is our superior."

Houston then spoke up and says, "Gentlemen, those are the
first wild Indians I evar saw and not being accustom to savage
ware fare and both of you are, I think it would be doing you
and your men especially great injustace for me to ta[ke the]
command." Said he, "Now give me a deciplined civ[iliz]ed
command and a deciplined enemy to fight I would redily take
command."

They insisted and he taken command,[8] and while this parly was going on the Indians kept up a continuous fireing and in the five or ten minutes thare was five or six of us wounded.

In the space between the Indians and Texians thare was six or eight chiefs all dressed in guada aray, one haveing on a cap mad from the face or mop of a buffalo with the horns still on and sticking straight up, with about ten yards of red ribon tied to each horn, another with a two story bee gum silk hat on his head with at least ten yards of each color, red, green, and blue ribon, one end of each tied round his hat the other end loose streaming in the air behind, another one had a green silk umbrilla streached over him, another that was kilt had on red top boots, blue cloth pants and coat with the coat hind part before and buttoned up behind, another had a cap dressed with feathers of diffrent wild fowls, eagle, hawk, and others with a row of silver spoons stuck in it and a bunch of peafowl feathers stuck in the center, and the rest of them was dressed equely as guada but those I have discribed show the stile.[9]

Those chiefs were runing back and fourth in the space between the two armies performing such feats of horsemanship as none but a Commanche, who is raised on horsback, can perform. Lying flat on the side of their horse with nothing to be seen but a foot and a hand, they would shoot their arrows under the horses neck, run to one end of the space, straighten up, wheele their horses, and reverse themselves, allways keeping on the opisit side from us. The line of warriors just behind these chiefs kept up a continuous fireing with their escopets doing no damage but they had som fine rifles taken at Linville and those done all the damage. While the parly was going on I noticed Henry McCulloch

[8] "Capt. Caldwell, in the bigness of his heart, rode out in front and moved that Gen. Felix Huston take command" (*ibid.*, p. 81).

[9] "As the long column marched across the prairie it presented a ludicrous sight. The naked warriors had tried to dress themselves in the clothing they had stolen. Many of them put on cloth coats and buttoned them from behind. Most of them had on stolen shoes and hats. They spread the calico over their horses, and tied hundred of yards of ribbon on their horses' manes and to their tails" ("Brazos," *Life of Robert Hall*, p. 49).

about half way the space and near whare those chiefs ware performing such feats of horsemanship, standing behind a small
mesquit tree trying, as he said afterwords, to git a fair pop at one
of those fine dressed gentlemen.

I was close to Ben and directed his attention to Henry saying
at the same time, "Henry is in a dangerous place."

Ben galloped of toward Henry and I saw a chief start towards
Ben, and I raised my gun and was in the act of shooting and had
a good bead on him when a ball struck me in the hand between
my for and middle finger, raingeing towards and lodging in or
near the rist joint, whare it remains to this day. When the ball
struck my hand it caused me to pull the trigger of my gun and
she fired, and at the crack of my gun the chief with the buffalo
cap on was seen to fall, his horse falling at the same time. My ball
had taken efect penetrating through the horse killing him dead
and braking the chiefs thigh, but when the the horse fell the chief
was seen to rise and hop of a few steps and while thus exposed old
John McCoy shot and kilt him. About this time the charge was
mad and thare was a hard fought battle over him, and thare was
ten or a dozen wariours lost their lives trying to carry of the
boddy of their dead chief.

The three officers was yet standing togeather when French
Smith seeing so many gitting wounded and takeing in the situation says, "Boys, lets charge them," and started of in a run, and
the whole company, suposeing the charge had been ordered by
an officer, charged after Smith. One of Burlesons men, Hutcheson
Reede, had come across to see what was causing the delay as
Burlesons command had become impatient, and Caldwell seeing
his men in motion, started of in the charge, and Burleson broak
back and ordered his men to charge round the point of timber.

Houston simply hollowed, "Charge," and filed in amongst the
croud.

The savages, seeing Caldwells men behind them and Burlesons
men on their right and all chargeing them, they ingloriously fled
leaveing everything but the horses they rode. After fireing my
rifle I was unable to reload it, and I consigned it to the holder at

the horn of my saddle and, having a brace of old Inglish brass mounted holsters, I drew one of them with my left hand and was of amongst the foremost in the charge.

Just before I arived at the place whare the Indians had first halted I saw an old Indian squaw standing by the side of her horse and the prisnrs dismounted and standing near by, and when the rought commenced this old mother of the forest, seeing the Texians in full chace after the Indians and them flying, sent an arrow through the negro girl killing her instantly, then turned to Mrs. Crosby shot her dead, then turned to Mrs. Watts shot her with an arrow but in such a hurry she failed to kill her but inflicted a dangerous wound in her breast and then ran for her horse, but received the contents of my holster before she could mount.

Reede did not return to his command but filed in to the charg, but did not go fare before his horse became unmanageable and, in trying to controle him, the bridle bit broak in the horses mouth and fell out. Haveing now no constraint the horse almost quit the ground and furious with rage, ran past me as though I had been standing still and drove into the thickest potion of the flying enemy, and he ran with the enem[y] for som peace and them sending arrows after him, he was hit with six arrows in the boddy and legs and finely his horse fell pearced through with a ball, and he was in the act of riseing to his feete when one of the hindmost savages shot him with a rifle, the ball passed through him entering near the right nipple and comeing out under the right shoulder blade.[10]

After dischargeing one of my holsters at the squaw that shot the prisnrs I returned it to the holster, drew the other one and, as I was rideing a good horse, I was soon up with the hindmost potion of the flying enemy, and as the Texians and Indians ware

[10] "Brazos," (*ibid.*, pp. 50–52) tells the story: "Here I witnessed a horrible sight. A Captain and one man rode in among the Indians. The Captain escaped, but I saw the Indians kill the private." However, later on he says: "We lost not a man, but seven were wounded."

Brown (*Indian Wars and Pioneers*, p. 82) says: ". . . Reed of Bastrop had an arrow driven through his body, piercing his lungs, though he lived long afterwards."

conciderable mixtup and a great many of the Indians dressed in citizens cloths, it was hard to distingush them apart.

I discovered one Indian som distance in the rear of the main force of the enemy and I urged my horse on and was soon up with the Indian. I raised my pistol and fired and the Indian fell from the horse, rolled over displaying a pair of larg flabby breasts that accounted for her being in the rear of som of the Texians as they had discovered her to be a squaw and passed on. It is difficult to distinguish the sexes of a flying enemy when both sexes dressed the same for she carried a bow and quiver but did not attemt to use it.

I put my empty pistol back in the holster, drew my belt pistol, a larg Deringer, and went on after the flying enemy. I arived on the bank of a boggy creek litterly bridged with packs, dead and bogged down horses and mules, and saw two Indians climeing the bank on the otherside, and fired at one and they both fell, but am not certain that I hit either of them for just to my right thare was six or eight guns fired at the same time that I fired.

My arms was now all emty and I was unable to reload so I sit watching the flying enemy and their persuers, and about seventy or eighty yards ahead of me I discovered Alsa Miller, C. C. Dewitt, and two or three others in full chace after a chief and his wife both on one horse and was crouding them close, and just ahead of the chief was five or six wariors. The chief saw that he would be overtaken and blew his whistle loud and the wariors all turned back, deturmend I supose, to die with their chief if nessesary, and when Miller and the other boys and the wariors had nearly met the other boys all fired with good effect each killing his man but Millers gun missed fire, but the other boys seeing thare was but one Indian left, thought Miller would take care of him haveing a repeateing rifle, hurried on to over take the chief.

The warior, seeing Millers gun had missed fire, rushed on to him and Miller haveing one of those old fashioned seven shooting rifles with a brass cylinder, about the size of a breakfast plate, sitting on the bretch of his gun, after fireing would have to revolve it with his hand, and this time being in a hurry, he failed to turn the cylinder fare enough to catch. Miller and the Indian met and when their horses heads passed each other the two mens legs almost touched and the Indian commenced to pull his bow-string, for he had already adjusted an arrow. Miller said he could see his bow begin to bend when he raised his gun and with a side swing hit the Indian on the side of the head staggering him back and knocking his bow clear out of his hands.

Now they ware both as good as unarmed but as quick as thought the savage snatched a handfull of arrows from his quiver and job[ed] them against Millers breast trying to stab him with them. By this time Miller had discovered the defect and remided it and shot the Indian dead. There is but a fe[w] men would have gone through such an ordeal wtih as mutch composure as did Miller, but he was a brave man, cool and deliberate, his pasion lay deepe and was hard to bring to the surface, but when it was raised he would face danger with more composure than any man I ever knew. Always smileing when his anger was highest, he was cautious, prudent and watchful, never allowing an enemy to git the advantage of him. He was generous to a fault and he and I was ever fast friends. A little incident occured the first time we ever met that mad us friends for life. Reader, please excuse this digression from the subject.

All this occured in about five minuts and I was still sitting on my horse whare I had been watching Millers fight with the Indian when I heared a noise behind me and turned my head and saw a horse fall and an Indian tumble of. When the horse fell I suposed the Indian was dead, but in a few moments she, for it was a squaw, gained a sitting posture, but I had nothing to shoot with if it had been a man armed, but I discovered it was a woman and also observed she had no bow and arrows.

I discovered she had been shot through both thighs and both thigh bones broaken and I stood and looked at her as th[e] dying horse had scrambled near her and died, and I was just going to ride of when I saw two men under full speede comeing towards me. Now I am going to relate a circumstance that makes shiver now, and I am going to show that the American race is not wholly exemp from acts of cruelty and barberism, for these two men comeing full speede was old Ezkel Smith and French

Smith, his son, they came near and discovered the wounded squaw and they halted. The old man got down, handed French his panting horse to hold, saying at the same time, "Look thare, French," pointing to the old wounded squaw with her long flabby breasts hanging down as she had recovered a sitting posture. He drew his long hack knife as he strode towards her, taken her by the long hair, pulled her head back and she gave him one imploreing look and jabbered somthing in her own language and raised both hands as though she would consign her soul to the great sperit, and received the knife to her throat which cut from ear to ear, and she fell back and expired. He then plunged the knife to the hilt in her breast and twisted it round and round like he was grinding coffee, then drew it from the reathing boddy and returned the dripping instrement to its scabard without saying a word.

French says, "Well, Father, I would not have done that for a hundred dollars."

"Done what," says the old man.

"Why, kilt a woman, a human being."

"That aint a human. Thats an injun and I come to kill Injuns, and all the rest has out run me and got away."[11]

He mounted his horse and they both galloped of after the croud, but I still sit thare on my horse a few seconds longer wondering if thare was another man in America that claimed to be civilized that would act so cruel. Smith claimed to be a Christian and had belonged to the Methodist church for 27 years and led in prayr meetings and exorted in public and was a noted class

---

[11] John H. Jenkins of Bastrop, who was in the battle, gave the following description of this event: "As was often the case some squaws were marching in Indian ranks, and one of them had been shot and lay breathing her last—almost dead as we came by. French Smith with most inhuman and unmanly cruelty, sprang upon her, stamped her and then cut her body through with a lance. He was from the Guadelupe . . ." (quoted in Joseph Milton Nance, *Attack and Counterattack* [Austin: University of Texas Press, 1964], p. 24n. 47). Nichols, who had lived in the same community as the Smith family and had been in other battles with them, was probably correct in stating that Ezekiel Smith, the father of French Smith, was the person who killed the squaw. The Smiths were strangers to Jenkins and he could have confused the two.

leadre, but the old fellow has long sence gone to reap his reward whare the woodbine twinethe and the wangdoodle mourneth for her first born.

I suposed I had been thare since I first arived near ten minuts when I discovered that my wound had commenced to bleede rapidly, and I turned and started back and saw a bolt of yellow silk streatched out on the grass and bushes about 40 yards long and about 12 inches wide. I alited from my horse, taken one end, raped the whole bolt around my wounded hand and started to mount my horse again, and for the first time [I] discovered that the foretree of my saddle had been pearced with a large escopet ball cutting both forks intirely in two leaveing nothing to hold the saddle togeather but the raw hide cover.

I rode on a peace farther and Brother Thomas call to me and I went to whare he was. He had just arived with a gourd of watter for Reede and th[e] doctor was comeing, and I saw Doctor Brown ex[tract the] arrows from him and dress his wounds. By [then thare w]as several of Reedes friends had come and they p[ut him] on a blanket and started to the point of timber to find a shade, for it was an auful hot day.

I and Brother Tom and the doctor went on togeather and when we arived at the timber we found Mrs. Watts suffering very mutch with the arrow still sticking in her breast, and the doctor tried to extract it, but she could not stand the pain. Just at this time David Darst rode up, and he was the brother of Mrs. Watts[12] and had been informed of her captivity. When the rout commenced he had passed some distance from her and went on in the chace hopeing to overtake and recapture her, and went on until he was satisfide she was not ahead and turned back hopeing to git some tideings of her. He now found her alive but seriously wounded, and he jumped of his horse, ran and kissed her, then proceded to cut open a bale of blankets that lay near by, spread

---

[12] Nancy Darst, David Darst's sister, must have been named Watts by a second marriage, for the Court Records of Gonzales County show that Nancy Darst married Thomas S. Mitchell in 1834. Brown (*Indian Wars and Pioneers*) also speaks of Major Watts' being killed at Linnville and of "his young bride" being captured (see note 4, this chapter).

Battle on Plum Creek

down a lot of them in a shade, and they all remooved her to it. They layed her down, and Dave held her hands, Brother Tom her head, and the doctor extracted the arrow after the third trial.[13]

The others that was wounded was Robert Hall in thigh, Henry C. Winchel in arm, James Gipson in shoulder, Mrs. Watts in breast, Hutcheson Reede in six places in boddy and legs and a rifle ball went through his boddy, the writer in the hand and two more slightly, both flesh wounds.

Late in the evening when most of the men had returned from th[e] chace, the officers picked out a suitable place to [camp] on the south side of the creek close to watter an[d a pr]arie, serounded on all sides but one with st[ands of] timber and dog-

[13] "Brazos" (*Life of Robert Hall*, p. 51) gives a different account—and a different maiden name: "A little further on I found Mrs. Watts. They had shot an arrow at her breast, but her steel corset saved her life. It had entered her body, but Isham Good and I fastened a big pocket knife on the arrow and pulled it out. She possessed great fortitude, for she never flinched, though we could hear the breast-bone crack when the arrow came out. She turned over on her side and bled a great deal, but she soon recovered. She was the wife of a custom house offiicer, and I think her maiden name was Ewing." This version appears only in *Life of Robert Hall*. Z. N. Morrell (*Flowers and Fruits in the Wilderness* [4th ed. rev., Dallas: W. G. Scarff and Co., 1886]) and Brown (*Indian Wars and Pioneers*) agree with Nichols that a doctor removed the arrow.

wood brush, opiset or a little below the main battle ground, and
ordered all the goods thare, and they chose another similar place
to correl the horses and mules in.

The next morning they appointed a commity to divide the
goods[14] according to quantity and quality and put them in just
two hundred and three piles, just the nomber of men inguaged
in the battle. I was lying in the shad and saw Brother John comeing in with a load of saddle trees, some ten or fifteen on his horse,
and I called to him to come by and he came up and I told him
that my saddle tree had been shot in two and ruined, and I wanted
him to pick out a good one from his lot and put the rigging of
of my old saddle on it for me which he did [for] the saddle trees
had been taken at Linville by the savages and was of Childresses
make.[15] I have rode that saddle tree ever since and now when I
ride a horseback I ride that same saddle tree. I have had it rigged
several times and it is still the same tree but looks [a] little the
worse for ware as it has been in almost constant use forty seven
years.

Thare was squads of men ariveing in camp all evening and
all night so that by the next morning I guess thare was five or
six hundred men on the ground. The comity appointed to divide
the goods, after all the packs had been opened and divided, taken
a bunch of knitting nedles and stuck them in the ground by the
side of each pile of goods with a slip of paper in each bunch of
nedles and they then proceded to stake for them. They placed
a man out side of the ring with his back to the good[s to] call
the role and thare was one man appointed to go [around and]
hollow out, "Whose is this pile," and point to the nedles, and
[the other man] would call som name and so on [until the last

14 "Brazos," *Life of Robert Hall*, p. 53, tells: "We captured the Indian pack
train. The mules were loaded with household furniture, wearing apparel, and
general merchandise. There were five hundred of these pack mules. The government had just received a supply at Linnville, and the Indians had captured
these. We hardly knew what to do with all this stuff, and we finally concluded
to divide it among ourselves."

15 Rice and Childress were saddlers in San Antonio and made the Hope Saddle-
tree. For some years before the Civil War they had a contract to furnish saddles
for the U.S. Cavalry. See National Archives and Records, Record Group No. 156,
War Department, Washington, D.C.

name] was called and the last pile of go[ods was gone. We used the same] way[16] in divideing the horses and mul[es. An animal was chosen and when a] name was called the man or his represen[tative then came] and roped his animal, and I drew the best sad[dle horse] that I ever rode. It was a natural pacer and Brother John roped it for me and said he wanted me to have an easy ride home as I was wounded.

After Dr. Brown of Gonzales extracted six arrows from the boddy and legs of Reede and drew a strip of silk clear through his boddy at the bullet hole, he was carried home on a litter and recovered and lived many years afterwards. All the wo[un]ded except him and Mrs. Watts was able to ride home horseback, and the prisnrs, nombering about thirty, mostly women and children save one little boy that judg Ballinger taken home with him,[17] was turned over to the Lipan Indians who retired with the prisnrs about a mile above us and had a big scelp dance that night.

I have written this lengthy sketch from notes taken on the ground by Brother Thomas on the statements of Mrs. Watts, and that lady said as herself, Mrs. Crosby, and the negro girl ware all tied on pack mules they ware frequently driven togeather while traveling so that they held conversation and by that means she learned both of their stories.

I have noticed one writer in writing on this campaign brands Caldwell with [cow]aredice for giveing up the command to Houston, and [says that it] was faught seven or eight miles northwest of Lockhart. He says here was concentrated the companies of Ben McCulloch, Henry McCulloch, Clark L. Owin, Jack Hays, John H. Moor, Wm. B. Dewees, Thomas Ward, Ed Burleson, Mathew Cladwell, Ad Gelispi, Kit Acklin, and others, leaving the impression that thare was so many companies that it tired him so he could not write all of them down. He says all these ware on the ground with their companies, Genl. Felix

---

[16] "The trophies, during the next day, were classified, numbered and drawn by lot" (Brown, *Indian Wars and Pioneers*, p. 82).

[17] "Brazos," in *Life of Robert Hall*, p. 53, wrote: "He found a little child, a boy, lying on the leaves by itself. The soldier brought it out, and it proved to be a child of the head chief of the Comanches. They brought it to camp, and old Judge Bellinger adopted it. The little Indian did not live but three or four months."

Houston in command, and prepareations ware makeing for the
fight "when I with my Austin company rode up,"[18] now here is
eleven men with companies besides himself, and as he says "others," now, according to miletary rules, thare was a ridgment
which is one thousand men and two companies over, and on a
peace further he says the fight opened with 200 Texians against
what they suposed 500 Indians, and on further he says they had
just started their pack mules and was prepairing to follow, leaveing the impresion that the Indians had been camped or halted
to rest and was just starting on their journey. Now thare had
been men doging after them and watching them all the way
from Linville, and they never halted to eat, sleepe, nor rest since
they left that place.

Now the facts are just as I have stated, two hundred and three
Texians against two thousand Indians, for after the battle I
talked with a squaw who was taken prisner and who said she
was the wife of Tuckalote, the chief who had been kilt with the
buffalo head cap on. She spoke the Mexican languag well and
said thare was when they started eighteen hundred wariors, one
hundred muletarees or horseless, and one head chief and twenty
subordinent chiefs, and seventy five women and children.

Now it was a bad guess when he said what they suposed to
be 5,000 Indians for they had been veriously estemated by the
people of Victory, Linville, and other places at from 8,000 to
5,000, and to show further the untruth of this writer, Ben nor
Henry McCulloch, Dewees, nor Owins had any companies. Henry McCulloch is still liveing near Seguin and can be seen or con-
sulted by letter and can be relied on.

I will cote a few paragraphs from another writer, Dewees,
who wrote on the same subject and also for the Texas Almanac
just to show how absurd som men will be in their writeing to
go before and inlightened people suposing it will be taken as
facts. Dewees says these Indians had larg quantities of human

---

[18] This writer was Z. N. Morrell. His *Flowers and Fruits in the Wilderness*
(see note 13, this chapter) was first published in 1872. He was a Baptist minister
and participated in many of the early Indian fights. He was in the Plum Creek
fight but not in the same group as Nichols.

flesh done up in their packs evedently to cook and eat.[19] Now I
will leave this with the reader to judg of its correctness after a
few facts. They had not kilt any person since leaveing Victory,
and thare did not take time to take anything but scalps. Admit
they did, that was 19 days before this fight, except Mr. Watts
at Linville and they took nothing of him but his scelp, this was
in August and common sence would teach us that any kind of
meat done up in a pack would have been rotten in that length
of time in hot weather. The Comanches was not canabels no
how, they eat mule, beef, not human flesh.

The same writer says in the same letter, in their bundles was
found vast nombers of young alagaiters which they ware carrying back with them, som thought as curiousities, others thought
it was to show to the balance of the tribe as proof that they had
gone down as fare as the cost. Now it is strange that a man of
sence would write such stuff and have it circulated amongst the
riseing generation. To convince my readers who knows no better
I will only say I have seen thousands of alegators of all sizes in
the tributaries of the Colorado River, San Saba, Pecan Buyo, and
Concho rite whare the Comanches of that day was born and
raised.

I have but one more quotation to mak and I will be through,
that is from a writer who is the son of an old vetren and who
has wrote a book intitled *The Rangers and Pioneers*,[20] and in
writeing an account of this battle he says ". . . one man from
Seguin, James Nichols, was shot between the fore and middle
fingers while in the act of shooting at an Indian, the ball was cut
out at the rist joint and as the wound healed the two fingers grew

---

[19] "Among the spoil which we took from these Camanches, we found large
portions of human flesh evidently prepared for cooking" (W. B. Dewees, *Letters
from an Early Settler of Texas*, compiled by Cara Cardelle [Louisville, Kentucky:
Morton & Griswold, 1852], p. 232).

Brown (*Indian Wars and Pioneers*, p. 79) also criticizes Dewees' account:
". . . the false statements in 'Dewees Letters From Texas' giving the credit of
fighting the Battle of Plum Creek to four companies of citizen volunteers, he
claiming to have been Captain of one of them, when in fact not one of such companies was in the fight or even saw the Indians."

[20] A. J. Sowell, nephew of Andrew Sowell and son of Asa J. L. Sowell.

togeather up to the first joint. He is still liveing and draws a pension, etc.", but one mistake he makes is the ball never was cut out but remains in my hand to this day.

The same writer in writing up Andrew Sowell says, Andrew Sowell kept with the chace until his horse was run down then collected a croud of Guadaloupe boys and set out for home. Bad time to set out for home on a run down horse, especially when theire was three or four hundred horses and mules with the spoiles of goods, etc. to be divided amongst the victors. The fact is, we remained on the ground two days and nights before we set out for home. Chin music goes a long ways with som of the late writers.

CHAPTER VII

*1841 Captain Hays Company. Fight with Indians on the
Guadaloupe River. Red Headed Prisner. Fighting a Duel.
A Runing Fight on the Head of the Hondo. Mexican Horse
Thieves Kilted.*

IN THE SPRING of this year the Comanche tribe became
very troublesom, especialy in the west in and around San Antonio, evidently thinking to take reveng on the people of that
place and vecinity for their defeat two years before and Captain
Callahan having married and settled down manifested no de-
sire for farther military servis as Guadeloupe County seemed
compairitively at peace with the redskins.

John C. Hays, a popular man and a good Indian fighter, concluded to raise a company for three months servis and endeaver
to drive the savages from the vecinity of San Antonio as they
scarcely ever was out of sight. He saw and talked with some of
the government officers and they ashured him they would do
all in their power to have an appropriation mad to pay off him
and his men for all servises that they would render.

Hays wrote me a note stateing that he had the promace of
pay for the servis and that if I was not ingagued he wanted me
to joine him as trailor and scout. He said he had enguaged som
Lepan Indians but they ware so treacherous he could place no
confidence in them without a white man constantly with them.

I being compairitively idle I repaired with Calvin Turner and
Joe Williams to the place of rendezvouse. We ware mustered in
to servis by a proper officer and went into camp below town near
the old mission Consception but was not long idle for in a few
days their was a band of Commanches said to be eighty in number headed by Yaller Wolf, the noted ware chief, mad a raid in
the vecinity of town driveing off horses, killing several Mexicans
and one negro sheepe hurder and takeing one white man prisner,
a red haired child of Erin, who was also hurdeing sheep.

This was done in the evening in broad daylight and the news reached our camp about three hours before day the next morning and about sunrise thare was sixteen of us in our saddles. I was put in front with two Lepan Indians to trail and Hays with fifteen of the boys following close on our heels, the rest of the company being out on detached servis, some hawling provision, others out on a scout.

We followed them so rapidly, som times in a fast gallope, that we overtaken them on the Guadaloupe River at what was then called the Pinta Trail Crossing, it is now the crossing on the road leading from San Antonio to Fredericksbourg.

Just as we rode upon the bank on one side the savages ware going up the bank on the other side and we opened fire on them, killing several and wounding others but they succeeded amidst a gaulling fire from our pieces in remooveing their dead. They mooved on to the top and over the hill out of our sight. We crossed over and galloped to the top of the rise.

They had haulted and formed in line of battle. We pored in to their ranks another volly and made them scatter. We then retreated back down the hill to reload but before we had finished reloading we looked and saw the top of the hill red with the savages.

When they saw us they raised the war hoope or yell and charged down towards us but seeing we did not flee but stood our ground, they charged half way down the hill, discharged their escopets and a perfect shower of arrows at us, wheeled their horses and galloped back, followed by loud yels from the Texians and a volly of bullets.

We reloaded as quick as possable and charged them in return. We charged half way down the hill that time,[1] receiving their fire as we charged, ariveing within sixty yards of their line, we fired and retreated as before with the savages in full chace as before and they fired and retreated.

Captain Hays then sent half his men to charge and draw them out and while their guns ware emty the other half would charge

---

[1] This charge of the Rangers was down the far side of the hill. The Indians and Rangers were charging each other back and forth over the top of the hill.

them. That plan worked well as the reserve ran in and kilt several and wounded the chief Yaller Wolf severly.

It was then too dark to charge them again and awaited their charge as we had two men wound[ed] severly and one slightly. Sam Luckey in left thigh slightly, Jack Pearson in the fleshy part of the right thigh with an arrow, Dave Larance in shoulder with ball.

Cal Turner, Joe Williams and myself was sent to the top of the hill to watch the manuvers of the enemy while the wounded ware taken care of. The savages did not seem disposed to fight any mor unless forsed to and as soon as it began to git dark the Indians bundled up and left under cover of night, leaveing us masters of the situation with a gret quantity of their accutrements and about thirty five horses which they had abandoned.[2]

The Irish prisner whom they forse to and carried off but who afterwards mad his escape and whose name was James Dunn reported that we kilt twenty three that they burried that night after the moon rose by cutting holes in them, filling them full of rocks and sinking them in a deep watter hole. He also stated that Yaller Wolf with thirty six of his men was wounded and that thirteen died from their wounds on their way out. This man had remarkeble red hair and when he returned he said that the bloody

---

[2] The story is also told by Sowell, in *Rangers and Pioneers*, pp. 57–58, who adds something more: "Sometime in 1842, Captain Jack Hays, with fifteen men, including Ad. Gillespie, Sam Walker, Sam Luckie, and the famous story-teller, Kit Acklin, fought his celebrated and most desperate battle with Yellow Wolf and eighty Comanche warriers, at the Pinta Trail crossing of the Guadalupe, between San Antonio and Fredericksburg, and, after a hand-to-hand contest and two charges, defeated them, killing and wounding about half their number, with a loss of one killed and three wounded, but without taking much spoils. Hays' report of the efficiency of the five-shooters used in these battles caused Mr. Colt to produce the six-shooter, and to engrave on the cylinder the ranger on horseback charging Indians."

The origin of the engraving on the Colt six-shooter is confirmed by Wilbarger, *Indian Depredations in Texas*, p. 290: "The fight with Yellow Wolf on the Pedernales, in which sixteen of this troop fought in open prairie seventy-five Comanches, will always remain one of the most remarkable episodes of border warfare to be found in the annals of any land. This was the first engagement with Comanches in which Colt's revolvers were used, and the engraving so familiar for many years on the cylinders of those of subsequent manufacture, was designed to represent this battle."

divels neither tortured, kilt nor ate him alive which he expected
them to do but actuely taken a fancy to him and treated him
with greate kindness but he said that they came within an ace
of drowning him in the river while attemting to wash the red
off of his hair which they taken to be paint. He said they would
scrub his head with sand and watter for hours at a time.[3]

On another occaision a band of the savages mad a raid and
stole and drove off a large bunch of horses but not being discovered at the time it was two or three days before the news
reached Hays. Nevertheless, he concluded to follow them thinking as they ware not persued at the start that after a few days
they would git carless and stop, rest and recruit.

After trailing two or three days my horse became lame and I
went back in line leaveing Joe Williams with the two Lepans
to do the trailing. One evening the trail became fresh and about
nine oclock one morning we come on their camp which they had
left that morning.

Captain Hays ordered every man to keepe his place in line
and make as little fuss as posable. If a man broak lines for anything he should fall in the rear of the line. Thare was one man
who was overbearing and boistrous, head long fellow and always
cursed and swore and always gitting mad when he could not have
things his way. His name I shal withhold for several reasons, one
of which is that he is still liveing and he and I the best of friends.

This man broak lines for som purpose and com galloping up
to the place he had left, tried to git in line, but the boys refused
him, saying, "Fall in the rear."

He kept trying to git in along the line until he reached whare
I was and said, "Let me in here, Jim."

I says, "Did you not hear the orders this morning."

[3] Sowell, in *Rangers and Pioneers*, p. 58, also told the story: "Before or after
this engagement, a ranger named James Dunn, whose hair was remarkably red
was captured by the Comanches and led away a hopeless prisoner, to their camp.
Strange to say, the murderous, bloodthirsty savages neither tortured, killed, or
ate him alive, which he thought they would do, but actually took a fancy to
him, treated him with great kindness, and, as Jim afterwards related, came within
an ace of killing him with kindness, or, rather, drowning him in Rio Frio while
attempting to wash the red (paint) from his hair."

He says, "Dam the orders, let me in!"

He was rideing a splendid horse with but one eye. He mad one or two unsuccessful attempts to git in and then squared his horse and mad a lung and crouded me out. About the time he got straight in line I punched his horse on the blind side with the but of my gun and the horse whirled round so rappied that he threw his rider and I saw no more of him until night.

The Indian sign was gitting quite fresh but as it was now sundown Captain Hays concluded to go in to camp and croud the enemy next day so we could have daylight for the attact.

Som of the mischieveous boys heard this fellow who we will call Dan cursing and muttering the most bitter oaths. They learned the facts in the case and John Rodgers, Cal Turner, Bill Deadman and Joe Williams got togeather and concocted a plan to have som fun. Just before we went into camp John Rodgers found a large poke stalk full of berries. He geathered som, put them in his shot poutch saying to the boys, "We can have som real fun with these." They let me in to their plans and I consented.

That night I received a chalange from Dan to fight him a duel at sun rise the next morning with our rifles. I excepted the chalange and chose the mode. We was to stand five paces apart with our backs to each other and was to wheel and fire between the words two and three. We chose our seconds. He chose Bill Deadman as his second and Joe Williams to load his gun. I chose Cal Turner as second and John Rodgers to load my gun.

It was warm weather and we both appeared on the ground with only shirt and drawers as did our seconds. While our seconds was masuering the ground and placing the combatents in position, Joe Williams and Rodgers went round behind som brush to load the guns. Williams loaded his gun with a heavy charge of powder and poke berries and Rodgers loaded my gun with a heavy charge of powder and penolie.

Now som of my readers may not know what we mean by penolie. It is corn parched brown and ground on a hand mill into corse meal and mixed with brown sugar. We rangers used a great quantity of them on scouts after the enemy. We seldom ever stoped to cook from morning til night and when we began to feel hungry and came to watter, take our tin cup half full of watter and stir som penolie into it and drink it. It keeps off hunger and greately assists in keeping off thirs.

You can amajon how a load of penolie dough would look shot on to a mans clothen and all know how poke berry juice would look on the bosom of a white shirt. Well, the men came back with the guns and handed them to us. We was in posision with our backs to each other and was to wheel and fire between the words two and three.

Bill Deadman counted the words one and two was said. We both wheeled and fired simultainously. He squirted the red juice all over my bosom and I landed my wad of penolie about two inches in front of the point of Dans left hipbone. When the guns fired I staggered and fell.

"Thare!" said Rogers, "You have kilt Nichols! Look at the blood!"

Dan cast his eys around and saw the blood.

"Dan is kilt too," said Cal. "Look at the food runing out at the bullet hole."

Dan felt of the place and got som of the panolie on his fingers, saw it and fainted. It taken som time to restore him to consciousness. When the[y] did the boys explained the whole matter to him saying it was all in a joke. Dan made acknowledgements to me and we were ever after that good friends but he gave the other boys Hail Columbia![4]

Now, reader, you can see what fun a set of rangers can have even when in close persuit of the enemy, not thinking or caring that in case we should overtake and fite the Indians it might be their time to go hence. We prepared everything in readiness for a fight or a chace at least and mounted and set off at a brisk gait

---

[4] The story of this duel was verified recently by Mr. Gerald DuBose, Victoria, Texas. His grandfather, Friendly DuBose, served as a Texas Ranger under Captain John H. Rogers, the same John Rogers who loaded Nichols' gun for the duel. Evidently Rogers told the story to the Rangers, as it was a favorite tale of Friendly DuBose, who passed it on to his son and grandson.

to overtake the Indians and in this we was not kept long in sus-
pence for we had not traveled mor than six miles when we
sighted the redskins just prepareing to leave camp. Their horses
all hobbled yet but brought up to camp. They ware camped
near the edge of a dence cederbrake.

Hays ordred a charge. We charged upon their emty camp
for the birds had flown. We never even got to fire a gun. They
ran into the breake, leaveing everything. We taken such of their
accuteriments as we chose, guns, bows, arrows, buffalo skins,
ropes, etc., and taken all the horses and returned to camp. We
narated it that we had recaptured the stolen horses and in a few
days the owners came in and carried them off.

We now had but little to do as the Indians had been defeated
in nearly every effort they mad to steal and plunder the setlers
as we kept out scouts in every direction and the redskins soon
learned this fact and would not venture to put in an apearance.
The time passed off with nothing mor to mar the peace and
quiature of the setlers.

Our turm of servis had now drawn to a close and we was mus-
tred out by a compatent officer and set out for Seguin. On ariveing at that place we learned thare had been occaisionly som
disturbanc, thare having been horses stolen and cattle would
come up with arrows sticking in them and som mocenson tracks
found, but the sign seemed to be done by som one on the Indians
credit.

In the spring of this year and while I was in the servis under
Hays, old Antonio Navaro opened up a large farm and stock
ranch som eight miles north of Seguin at som large spring on
the San Jaronamo and on a league of land owned by him. At
the time I speak of he had near two hundred acres in a farm and
kept from 12 to 15 peone or slave families on his ranch besides
from 20 to 30 single men, all Mexicans. He had near three thousand head of cattle and five or six hundred head of horses. Such a
place naturely drew a motly croud and small squads of Mexicans of doubtful carecture was constantly going and comeing
but while the old man Navaro kept controll of the ranch every-

thing went on like clock work, straight and honest, for if thare was an honest Mexican he was one. One incident will proove that assersion. He went [on] the Santefe expedition. They ware all taken prisners and marched to Mexico and while thare confined in a close prison, the Mexicans discovered that he was a Mexican and the authorities offered him his liberty if he would cut the Lone Star buttons off his coat. He said he would die in prison before he would disgrace the caus of Texas.

After Navaro had gotten everything about his ranch in good working order, the Santa Fe Expedition was mad up and he joined it with the above result. He left the controll of the ranch with his son young Antonio Navaro, a plasure loveing young man who had a fandango nearly every night at the ranch.

Thare was one Chri[s]tova Aroulga⁵ whoes wife was imployed as head cook but her husband was not imployed at the ranch but had four of five men in his imploy and going here and thare claiming to be tradeing but mad the ranch his head quarters. He always carried a bow and quiver full of arrows besides his escopet. He would, as we found out afterwords, go to San Antonio, shoot an arrow into a cow to make Indian sign, steal six or eight head of good horses, take them east to the Colorado or Brazos Rivers and sell or swap them for good American horses, take them back to San Antonio and sell them for money, start out a gain and repeat the same thing. He had been suspected and watched but had not been caught. They mad a raid or two on Seguin. In that way they could make first rate Indian sign but never takeing more horses than they could ride off so they could scater one in a place.

One light moon they swooped down on us and stole six or eight horses and amongst the rest Captain Callahans fine saddle horse, of corse, that riled the Caps feeling. Next morning Callahan, Milford Day and myself walked round looking for sign.

Callahan says, "Boys, I believe them horses has gone to the ranch. Now either of you can trail a single horse over worse

---

⁵ The name was probably "Arouba," a common Spanish name. Later in the story Nichols spells it "Arouba."

ground than this and I want you to see if I am not right."

So Milford and I started on a horse track a piece. We trailed them about five miles and we was not over two hundred yards apart at any time. We found whare they had all come together and makeing directly for the ranch. We turned back, raised a croud, Callahan, Milford Day, John Nichols, Jim Roberts, Hardin Turner, Cal Turner, Joe Williams, John and Asa Sowell, Andrew Sowell, myself and Lee.

We struck the trail whare we had left it and followed on to the ranch. We mad no inquiries at the ranch for fear of raising suspicion but passed on up the creek and struck the trail above the ranch and followed on up the creek and on to Yorks Creek Ridge.

We saw that they ware makeing directly for what we then called the big thicket. We followed the trail to the edg of this thicket. We found a newly cut trail into the thicket. Callahan took the lead, the rest of us close on his heels. Near the middle of this thicket headed a deep ravine in a small prairie containing good grass.

We had traveled this trail near two miles when we came in sight of this prairie containing twelve or fifteen acres. We mooved on causiously and soon discovered a bunch of horses close hobbled and down the gulley at the edg of the brush we discovered a smoke riseing. We knew that was their camp.

We alited, tied our horses, crawled up with in thirty steps of the fire before we could git a fair view of them. Thare ware five or six men sitting round the fire eateing supper. The sun was just setting. We each picked out his men and Callahan was to give the word.

Says he, "Take good aim, boys. Fire!"

All fired about the same instant and fiv[e] Mexicans fell dead. Two or three jumped to their feete and ran off. One of the men that ran of was Arouba, unhurt. The other two, one we never knew who he was or whare he went. The other was a little Mexican we all knew well. His name was Sancho Cabines.

We walked by the fire and took a look at the dead but did not tarry long as it was giting dark. We rounded up the horses, 12 or 15 in nomber includeing them stolen from Seguin the night before, and set out for home.[6] That broak up the band. About ten da[ys] after this, myself, Milford Day, John Nichols and Jim Roberts was all on a camp hunt in the vecinity of this camp and concluded to go by the camp and see what had become of the dead boddies and effects and down to the spring to git water for ourselves and horses.

We had frequently heard that neither wolves nor buzzards would eat a dead Mexican and we wanted to see if this was so. We struck the trail entering the thicket, went on to the camp and found every thing just as we had left them ten days before, tin cups, coffee pots, saddles, bridles, blankets, dead Mexicans and all as we had left them. After looking until satisfide we turned to go to the spring som three hundred yards down the hollow. When near the spring we heard a voice call to us to come thare. We halted, looking round in the brush, we saw Sancho, the little Mexican that had ran of but had been wounded. We crauled through the brush to him and thare I beheld the aufulest sight that my eys ever beheld before or since. He had been shot in the bowels and in the neck. He was litterly a pile of worms. It was warm weather and I am satisfide thare was a bushel of worms in, on and around him and him still alive and able to hollow to us. He comence to beg and implore us to kill him out of his misery, knowing that he could never recover as the maggots ware working all through his intrils.

Two of the boys whoes names I withhold says, "Lets end his suffering but let him die with a full belly."

We gave him as mutch meat and bread as he would eat which

[6] Sowell (*ibid.*, p. 193) also told of horsethieves: "About this time, Mexican horse-thieves, as well as Indians annoyed the settlers, and Captain James H. Callahan and his rangers used every exertion to catch them, but for some time were unsuccessful; but finally they were trailed to their hiding place by Milford Day, who was a splendid scout and trailer. Their location was in a large and very dense thicket, cut through by a deep and rugged gulley. This place was about eight miles northeast from Seguin, on York's Creek. Callahan, with a portion of his men, penetrated this thicket, and surprised them in their camp, which was near the deep gulley."

he devoured equel to a bitch wolf suckling eleven pups. We then gave him as much water as he would drink.

He then renewed his petitions to be dispached and said. "Shoot me in the head while I hold by hands over my eyes."

He put his hands up over his eyes and bowed his head to his knees and heard the report of two guns and was no more. That prairie is called Rogues Prairie and the gully is called Rogues Hollow to this day.[7] Old Araubea[8] was after wards captured by Lee with som stolen horses near San Antonio and while on his way to Seguin with his prisner halted at the Sebola[9] to take refreshment, he saw a band of Mexicans swooping down on him to rescue the prisner. Lee took in the situation at a glance, shot his prisner, mounted his horse and mad his escape.

The remainder of this year the war seemed to be at an end. The marauding bands of Indians had sceased their opperations and the Mexicans had mad no attempt to regain Texas. Everything like ware seemed to be lulled into a perfound and peaceful slumber and Soft Peace had perched upon the standered of our passed success and was huming a lullaby to suthe and soften the cares of our sleepeing wariors who knew nothing of the dark red cloud of war which was fast geathering and rolled up by the dusky sons of Mexico and which was soon to burst upon the devoted heads of the drowsy sleepers and cause Soft Peace to spread her wings and fly weepeing away.

[7] Sowell (*ibid.*, p. 194) told the story only slightly differently: "Near the spring, where the wounded Mexican was killed, there was a round rocky hill, with a grove of live oaks growing on its top, and there the Mexican was buried; and that place to this day goes by the name of the 'Rogues' Grave' and the place where they fought is called the 'Rogues' Hollow'."

[8] Here Nichols gives the Mexican's name yet another spelling. But the pronunciation of any of these variations would be very much the same.

[9] This would have been Cibolo Creek, which runs north and east of San Antonio.

CHAPTER VIII

1842 Raid by General Vascos. Raid by General Woll. Campain of 1842. Battle of Salado (Salow). Dawsons Massacree. Escape of Alsa Miller and Woods. Battle of the Hondo. Summervills Campain.

❧ IT HAD NOW BEEN about six years sence the Mexican government had attempted an invasion of Texas with their army but still claimed ownership and had kept up a constant warfare through their Indian allies. In the spring, the 7th of March, Gen'l Vascos, then commanding the Mexican forces at Matamoras, made a decent on San Antonio with twelve hundred vetrian troops,[1] led on by desineing men, two of whom I will mention, John N. Seguin, who had done signal service at the Battle of San Jacinto with a company of rancharoes in behalf of Texas and kept on doing good servises in watching the retreeting foe and reporteing their manuvers to head quarters. He was called on to inter the remanes of the fallen heroes of the Alamo which he responded to but who had turned traitor and had left Texas and all his larg posesions mostly land and taken a colonels comision in the Mexican army but who after many years sneaked

---

[1] On the morning of March 5, 1842, General Rafael Vásquez appeared on the outskirts of San Antonio with an army variously estimated from three hundred to one thousand soldiers. A scouting party of Texans from Captain Jack Hays' frontier defenders met a courier from Vásquez who bore a white flag and a message to the Texans demanding surrender of San Antonio and promising protection and immunity to all who did not resist. Since Captain Hays had only about a hundred men with him he decided to evacuate the town and by late afternoon most of the Texans had left San Antonio. The news of the Mexican army's arrival quickly spread throughout Texas and groups of "Minute Men" and volunteers were formed in many communities; however, by the time most of these reached the San Antonio area Vásquez had withdrawn and was on his way to the Rio Grande, having left San Antonio the morning of March 7.

Yoakum (*History of Texas*, II, 349) and Nance (*Attack and Counterattack*, p. 27) give the date of Vásquez' arrival in San Antonio as March 5. John Henry Brown (*History of Texas*, [2 vols., St. Louis: L. E. Daniell, 1892], II 212–214) gives the date as March 6. Nichols must have been thinking of the arrival date of the volunteer units of Texans when he said March 7.

back into Texas and claimed a pension under the law granting
pensions to old Texas vetrens and had his name placed by the
side of som of the men who he faught against at the Battle of
Salado and continued to draw the pension until his death.

The other was Antonio Periz, another noted Mexican leader,
who commanded a company under Santa Anna and assisted in
the massacree at the fall of the Alamo and who was left to garison
the place by the dictator, but after the occurance he was con-
cidred by som a friend to Texas and a good citizen. He remained
with us and done som good Indian fighting until 1840 when he
left Texas for the same purpose that Seguin did, a commission
as Col. in the Mexican army.

These two men had large landed estates and thare was suits
pending in the court at San Antonio to confiscate their lands,
and suposeng that court was in session at that place, it being the
time for the regular session, hence the raid by Gen'l Vascos, they
swooped down on the town and unsuspecting citizens about dark
when the town was an easy prey.

On their arivel they learned that court was not in session
owing to some unavoidable cause. They also learned that the
court would not convein until the 11th of the following September, and haveing no other buisnes to transact after sacking and
pillageing the town, takeing some goods and chattles as they
chose, set out on their return.

This news flew down the country almost with the swiftness
of the wind and spread from one settlement to another and once
more the call to arms was sounded a long the border to repell
Mexican invasion. This call was as ever promply obeyed by the
brave pioneers of the country and in about 14 hours there was
about one hundred and forty men on the march for the seen of
action with our old war horse Caldwell in command.

We arived at San Antonio to find to our chargrin that the
enemy had left the place. They had avaperated into thin vapor
and was being wafted on their course by the zepheries that faned
the rich prairies and the soft cool evening breeze that waved the
tall grass in their rear. They ware gone, Caldwell concluded.
Their suden flight without accomplishing anything or doing

any damage save the robing of the town, said he, "This must all be a ruse and they are hidout some whare to await the comeing of troops and then rush forth from their hideing place and make another Fanins defeat of us. So, boys, lets serch for them." Next morning we took up the line of march of their trail keeping out scouts on both sides but they war shure enough gone. We followed them to the Noeses River[2] and found that they had crossed that river full three days in advance of us, so we turned and retraced our steps back again.

Thare ware all sorts of conjectures about the object of this raid but none could guess aright and finding the real object unfathemable, we returned hom and disbanded, every man going his way.

But for days thare war squads of men ariveing from diferent potions of the country. Thare was one company from Montgumrey County about thirty in nomber arived at Seguin before we had returned, but learning that the enemy had retreated and that Caldwell was in pursuit, and that their servises would not be neaded, they concluded to go in to camp and rest their horses before returning. They went into camp near whare I had one hundred and six bee gums and commenced to assault them. They had been robed later in the fall leaveing only honey enough for them to subsist on through the winter and at this time of yeare they had very little honey. They went in to 6 or 8 of them and found no honey. It was almost too mutch trouble to prise the heads off and they taken an ax and split the gums open but got very little honey for their trouble. When I returne[d] the company had left for home and left me but six bee gum[s] whole.

While thare in camp they tried it seemed to do all the devil-m[ent] that lay in their power to do. They pressed all the corn they cou[ld] use and would carry out corn in sacks, pour it down on a blanket for their horses to eat and sit off ten steps, and when our hogs came up to help the horses eat the corn the men would shoot them down.

I had a large guinea sow and a great favorite, she had ten

[2] The Nueces River rises southwest of San Antonio and empties into Nueces Bay near Corpus Christi.

pigs in a bed near by. She came up near the horses and they shot her down leaveing the pigs to starve being not over a week old.

They kilt several beeves while thare in waste and the morning they left they kilt a cow for the widow Smith that had a calf in the pen four days old taken four ribs out and left the balance at the gate to stink. I don't know which would have served us the worst, the Mexicans had they come on or these American braves. After we ware rid of the Mexican army and those braves, everything seemed to lull down into a perfect forgitfulness. Vascos and the excitement he had created was soon forgotten. Had we known the real object of this raid, while soft peace was pearched upon our standered we would have been makeing preparations for war and not been charmed into sleepy idleness by her warbling these lines.

> Once more soft peace spread ore the land,
> Her wide streached balmy wings,
> And brings glad tiding in her hand
> And thus in her low chant she sings:
> Rest wariors, rest thy weary limbs
> On the soil thy blood and deeds made free,
> While the flaiming sword and cherubims,
> Guide the portals after me:
> Rest wariors, rest in slumbers charms.
> Duty makes troubles you must forego,
> Eare long you may hear the call to arms
> To repel the sons of Mexico.[3]

Gen'l Vascos having been remooved from the command at Matamoras and Gen' Adrian Woll put in his stead, now according to previous arangement made to the satisfaction of those two traitors, Seguin and Periz, accordingly on the 11th of September Gen'l Woll with eighteen hundred vetran troops and a battery of six pieces, two morters, two sixes, and two long nines made a decent swooping down on the town of San Antonio. Headed by those two reinegades and in broad daylight about 11 oclock in the morning, captured the town and with it the whole court, judge, lawyars and juryman with a few of the most proma-

---

[3] We have not been able to locate a source for this poem. Evidently it is Nichols' own composition.

nent citizens against whome those two traitors had a hatred, destroying all the papers in their cases and laying a contribution of the town for the suport of this victorious army and put out guards around the town with orders to shoot any man who attempted to leave the town, but the ever watchfull and viligent Erasmo, Deaf Smith,[4] who was up to any emurgency, mad his escape and carried the news to the Texians at Seguin and Gonzales. Again the news spread like wild fire and once more the gallent Caldwell, Hays, Callahan, the McCullochs, Fryer, Burd, and other, whoes gallentry has never been sullied, rallied their chosen and ever ready and willing but now idle scouts and rangers around them. The place of rendizvouse was at Seguin, and Caldwell hastened to that place sending out men to recruit—John Archer, Arch Gipson, Isham Jones, Clem Hinds, Alsa Miller and others and all night long men ware buisy makeing preporations once more to meete the dusky sons of Mexico on the battle field. All night long men ware comeing in and but few slept that night as cleaning up arms, moulding bullets, and cooking provisions was in order. Horses ware scarce as but few had suplied themselves sin[ce] the last Indian raids, and two men, my father and Dave Runnels, fought over an old stray horse each wanting to ride him on this campaign such was the zeal of the fronteermen in those days.

It was on this wise, while the Indians ware makeing raids in that vacinity, they abandoned an old paint horse which had given out and after lanceing him severly thinking he would die left him standing on their trail. The men following the trail thought

---

[4] This should be John W. Smith of San Antonio. There has always been confusion of these two Smiths. Because of his part in burning Vince's Bridge at the Battle of San Jacinto, Erastus ("Deaf") Smith was better known to most Texans of that time. He died November 30, 1837. John W. Smith had served as one of the guides for the Texans under Stephen F. Austin and under Ben Milam during the siege of San Antonio in the fall of 1835 and the Battle of Bexar, or Battle of San Antonio, in December, 1835. He was the first mayor of San Antonio under the Republic of Texas as well as the first county clerk of Bexar County. He carried one of the last messages from William Barret Travis out of the Alamo on March 3, 1836, and delivered it to the Consultation being held at Washington-on-the-Brazos where the Texas Declaration of Independence was being written. He died January 13, 1845, while a member of the Congress of the Republic of Texas at Washington-on-the-Brazos.

him not worth takeing any trouble with but a weeke afterwards Father saw him, taken him home and doctored his wound and turned him out again.

He mended so rapidly that in a few weeks he refused to be caught. Runnels had caught him and rode him a while one day but now the old horse was wild, wooly, fat, and sassy.

That evening Father says, "Jim, go and catch Old Paint for me. I want to go too."

I got several of the boys to go with me and we roped him on the prairie, braught him in, and tied him to Fathers gate post, and Father commenced makeing prepareations to go, moulding bullets, etc. Runnels had been out hunting the horse at the same time but missed him.

He came by in the evening, knew the old horse, he untied the rope, and was going to lead him off saying, "I am going to ride Old Paint myself."

Father walked out and says, "If you do, you will have me to whip first," and jerked the rope out of his hand.

Dave says, "I can do that dam quick."

Father says, "You are a dam liar."

They said a few words and went to quarling then hit a few licks and went to fighting. They fought near a half hour, and it seemed that neither was going to hollow.

By this time thare was at least twenty men standing round, som hollowing, "Hurah!" for one, and som "Hurah," for the other.

Milford Day stoo[d] over them with his pistol in hand saying, "If any man to[u]ched [them] he was his meat."

Still neither hollowed. When it seemed they was both so exausted that neither could hollow Milford and I parted them. Father bit off two of Daves fingers and a scollop out of one of his ears. Dave scratched and gouged Fathers face and eyes so that they both looked like a chawed calfrope when the fight was over. The next day neither of them was able to go on the campaign and another man, H. L. Cronn, rode the horse.[5]

---

[5] Nance (*Attack and Counterattack,* p. 342) gives the following version: "A

By this time thare had collected near two hundred men. Caldwell, knowing the mean deeds and outrages commited on the citizens the spring before by those men living farther east and did not want a repetition of such low degradeing acts so he apointed men all along the line of march to kill and barbycue beef for their benifit. Brother Solomon and old man Dunken at the bridg accross San Marcos, and he apointed Brother Thomas and Jim Alley at Col. Kings, Brother John and Milford Day at Seguin with instructions to keep constantly on hand a good suply of barbycued beef so that when a squad of men came a long way they would have nothing to do but ride up to the scaffel, fill their wallets and go on.

He also left instructions for all squads of men to ride rapidly without halting until they joined him, but one company of 26 men arived about three oclock in the evening, halted at the scaffel, helped themselves, turned off under some spreading liveoaks and went into camp.

After the boys had delivered Caldwells message to hurry up one of the men said, "Caldwell bedamed! If he can whip the Mexicans before we git thare itul be all right. If he cant he must wait ou[r] motion." They then demanded bread to go with beef saying, "We cant eat this fat beef without bread."

The boys told them that bread stuff was scarce, and the women and children needed all they had.

One man who seemed to be leader says, "Now, lookehere, if you have got a peck of meal and no more you had better bake it and throw it in sight before you suffer something worse."

Johns wife went to bakeing bread for 26 hungry men. After they had received the bread they demanded milk and butter to go with their bread and beef. They stayed thare all night and demanded the same for breakfast.[6] Consequently they never

---

stray horse which happened to be in town, was the cause of such a lively dispute that neither disputant was able to go at all."

[6] "During the night additional volunteers came in. The people of the town appeared to be very kind, but were very much imposed upon by some of the volunteers who showed 'their patriotism by infringing upon the rights of the citizens,' by seizing whatever of their property—beeves, sheep, and corn—they assumed would be necessary to their campaign" (Nance, *ibid.*, p. 343).

joined Caldwell until the clash of arms had been hushed and the
smoke of the battle had been wafted fare away over the prairie
by the evening breeze. Such I believe is found in every age.

Caldwell took command of all the forces and about one oclock
we set out on the march. We advanced to the Cibola, we halted
thare, and Caldwell sent Deaf Smith[7] with two men to reconoiter
and if posable find out whare the enemy had quartered and what
kind of position he had, and the advantages if any could be taken,
telling Smith at the same time that he would find him at the
crossing of the Salado.

Smith went on to the outskirts of town and posted his men
saying, "I will be back to you in the morning one hour before
day."

It was then after midnight. He found a favorable oppertunity
and passed the sentenels, went in to town changed his cloths
and put on some Mexican citizens cloths and stalked down the
row of tents talking with several of the subordenent officers that
was already up. He asked to be shown to Gen'l Woll's headquarters, as soon as he could be admitted, stateing that he had some
news to impart to the General privetly. The officer taken Smith
by the arm, led him to the Gen'ls headquarters and called him
up telling him thare was a citizen that had something of news to
impart. The Gen'l rose, dressed himself but seemed an age at it,
but received Smith very courtiously telling him to be seated and
that he was ready to hear him.

Smith stated that the news had reached town that thare was a
company of Texans on their way to attack him and that by noon
today they would reach the Salado seven miles from town. While
they ware talkeing Smith saw that day was breakeing and a co-
cinera or cook came in with coffee. While drinking their coffee
Woll asked him if the nomber had been stated.

Smith said, "Yes, it was stated thare was about two hundred."

"Two hundred!" echoed the General. "Why that would not
make a breakefast for our boys." Continued he, "Are you afraid
to go among them."

Smith said, "No!"

[7] See note 4.

He says, "Then git you an interpeter," thinking Smith by his speech was a full blood Mexican, "and go and tell them they need not put themselves to the trouble to come any farther. Tell them to choose them a position, and I will come out thare to-morrow morning and bring them in myself. The dungeons of Perote are nearly emty, and I would like to fill them with this gang of coyotes. Tell them I will be thare at sunrise tomorrow morning. Now dont stop until you have fulfild my orders."

Smith made a low bow and left the Markee and doffed his Mexican suite and doned his own, went back to his comrades, they mounted and set out for the command. Caldwell remained on the Cibola that night thinking reinforsements would arive.

After supper som of the boys had their blankets spread down [and were] playing cards. Others were in groops singing ware son[gs] and ditties. Others thare ware wrestling, running foot [races] or jumping. It was a fine moonlight night when [all at] once the bugle sounded for us to come togeather. [We] could not amageon what was up. We all geathered [round] the Captains fire.

Caldwell made us a short speech explai[ning] the call, then introduced Revrend Z. N. Morral who stat[ed] in a few brief remarks that himself and Parson Carroll [wan]ted to offer up their prays in behalf of the men before they i[ngua]ged the Mexican army in deadly combat, for, said Carroll, his petition tomorrow night may be the last night on earth for som [of] us. Parson Carroll sang and prayed and Morral preached a short but very appropriate sermon.

The guarde was chosen an[d] put under the command of Isham Jones as Sergent and the rest of us spread our blankets and the camp was soon rapped in that silent slumber so much injoyed by a tired soldier. Early the next morning we resumed our march for Salado. We halted for a few hours at noon on the Rociea[8] in hope of som recruits would join us but in vain and reached the Salado about four oclock in the evening.

Smith and his two companions ware already on the ground.

[8] This is the Rosilla Creek between the Cibolo and Salado creeks, east of San Antonio.

We halted and Smith gave Caldwell the detailes of his reconitre in the enemys camp, as above written. Caldwell delivered the same in a short speech to the men.

Smith, Caldwell, Hays, and the other officers set out up the creek to pick out a suitable position. After serching the creek on both sides they agreede on a position about two miles above the crossing on the east side of the Salado Creek. They returned and we mooved up and posted ourselves in position just as the sun was setting.

I will here discribe the ground for the better understanding of my readers. The creek itsself was a strong barier against invasion in our rear, being from thirty to forty feete wide and from 8 to 12 feete deep, extending from a half mile above our position to the same distance below with a steep bluff on the west side, the ground extending for probabley a mile in a low brushy ridge west, on the east side was a low bottom thickly set with large pecan and elm timbers and an emence groath of under brush and out at the edge of this bottom which was near forty yards wide was a narrow slip of prairie, say twenty yards wide, at the east side of this prairie was a bluff verying from seven to twelve feete high. On top of this bluff and eastwardly lay a high but leavel mesquit flat with hear and thare a large mesquite tree. The ground beyand rose graduly for half a mile to the top of the divide between the Salado and Salatrio which was a leavel hogwallow prairie with here and thare a mot of liveoakes or mesquite timber, otherwise open prairie.

This discription will hold good for the whole length of our line. Thare was a deep brushy ravine ran into the creek above us and a deep wide ravin with but little brush but concidrable elm and mesquit timber on its banks. These two ravines headed up near the top of the devide something over 80 yards apart and spread out in their course to the creek and emtied about five hundred yards apart.

As I before stated, we took our position just at sundown. We tied our horses in the timber in our rear and established our camp fires. The guard was drawn for the next day and night and the writer, as Sergent, given command of them. Caldwell posted

Hays with his spy company at and below the mouth of the upper ravine and posted me with the guard, thirty men, at and above the mouth of the lower ravine[9] and he taken the center with the main force. Thus our line extended about five hundred yards. The balance of the night was spent in cooking, eating, and gassing concerning what each would do on the morrow.

That night Smith was sent back to town or rather went without orders to deliver the message to Gen'l Woll that the Texans had excepted his chalange and had taken a position and was in waiteing for his lordship to make the attact, but was back in camp soon after midnight with a message from Woll that we would not have to wait long for promply at sun up the next morning he would be prepared to take us in out of the weather.

About two hours before day, fires were kindled all along the little strech of prairie against the imbankment and coffee made and beef roasted. Then could be heard the merry laugh and the greeting of each other as to how their puls beete. On the occaision I confess I was not in a very merry moode.

I mused thus. I may be kilt or wounded today and not a single relative to console me. I had a father, three brothers, four brother-in-laws, and three step brothers, and not one of them in this expedition and I felt lonely. Its true I had plenty of friend that would do all in their power in case of need. It was not so at the battle of Plum Creek whare I was wounded. I had my father, two brothers and two brother-in-laws by my side, never all leaveing me alone for a single instant but now it was different. I was serounded by only friends.

I was thus museing when Parson Carroll walked up to the guarde fire said he, "Brother Morrel and I have agreed to offer up our petitions to him who holds the destines of his people, and if you will call the guard togeather we will have prayr."

I done so and he prayed fervently for victory and a deliverance from the mighty host of the enemy who was soon to attack us. The most of the men seemed to pay strict attention.

---

[9] Nance (*Attack and Counterattack*, p. 350) states: "A Texan guard of twenty men was assigned to occupy this ravine in case of attack," but he does not give the names of those in the guard.

About an hour before day Caldwell ordered Hays with his spy company to town to draw the enemy out. Just as the bony gray eyed morning began to peepe, they heard the town all alive with drums and fifes and soon they beheled 400 dragoons come dashing up the road towards them. Hays turned his eyes to his men and saw their faces all kindled up with the joy of battle.

"Zowns!" said he, "Thare is quite an odds, 400 to 40, but let them come on."

But they halted out of range to await the comeing of the infantry and battery. Hays led them on and crossed the creek half mile above Caldwells position whare thare was a shallow ford and on up to the top of the ridg. When Hays wheeled his men under cover of the thick timber and took his position the Mexicans marched on to the crest of the hill, filed to the right, marched to the opening between the heads of the two ravines, displaying his whole force in full view of Caldwells men. They planted their battery, six pieces, two twelve inch morters, two long nines and two sixes.

The sun had climed the farther side of the hill and was peeping over seemeingly to see what was going on between the combatents. The Mexicans opened fire on us with grape canister and round shot, cuting the limbs and brush from the timber at least thirty feete above our heads but to the great anoiance of our horses. The falling limbs, som of which was as large as a commons mans thigh, falling on and around them caused them to rear and plunge and som few broake loose.

They kept up this fucilade for near an hour, fireing each piece at the rate of five shots [a] minute, when they sceased for a few minuts and was appearently holding a consultation, then opened fire again with new [v]igor, this time lowering their shots graduly until they commenced to cut the grass and even the dirt from our imbankment but still doing us no damage. They kept this up for probely another hour.

Seeing they could not dislodg us they mad a charge with their infentry as they saw they could do no good with their cavelry. They charged down the slope into the flat som forty yards from our imbankment, halted and formed their intire infentry, about twelve hundred, into platoons. Then formeing an oblong circul covering our intire line and traveled around that circul by platoons. As they would come round in a run nearest our lines, they would fire by platoons and keepe on in a run round the circul. When they would arive on the back line farthest from us they would reload, still traveling around the circul.

We soon found out that they taken no aim from hearing their balls pass so fare above us. We would crawl to the top of the bank and fire and it was seldom a Texas rifle fired that thare was not one seen to bit the dust. The Texans was picking them of so fast at every round that they refused to charge round the circul.

Then could be seen Seguin, Periz and other officers urgeing them on by slaping them with the flat side of their sabers. After carrying on this kind of warfair for an hour without doing us any damage except wounding one man, Jesse Zumalt, they withdrew with a los of twenty five kild dead and fifteen wounded so bad they was not taken off the field.

After parleying for half an hour, Woll dismounted all his cavelry, formed his intire force and marched down the slope in grand military stile, displaying about ten stand of colors with their drums beateing, their fifes, their bugles blowing a charge. It was a grand sight as every man could be planely seen as they marched down the hill, in all som over eighteen hundred. Seguin had command of the dismounted cavelry and was marching down the upper ravine but in line with the main force. The whole under command of Gen'l Woll himself.

I did not dream of what was in store for me and my thirty one men, called the guard. Cordova, the man that had figured so conspickously around Nacogdoches and whom Burleson had given such a brushing on Mill Creek, had just arived and had joined Woll with about one hundred Boluxie Indians and Woll had assigned him to the lower ravine with instructions to march down the bed of the ravine and if posable gain the rear of the Texans so they could have us between two fires.

While our attention was drawn to the grand display made by Woll, one of my men heard some nois in the ravine above us and

Battle on the Salado

mounted the bank and made the discovery of Cordova and his
men on all fores creeping down to the bed of the ravine, and he
motioned me, I went and saw the same.

I emediately formed my men into four platoons, telling them
not to all fire but take it in turns, always keeping some guns
loaded. I formed my men in front of a gap in the bank, telling
them as the enemy came in sight to fire which they did before
discovered by the enemy. At the firs fire the Indians rose to their
feete, yelling and faught like demons. We had the advantage of
the ground as we could part of us be behind the bank. They
charged to the top of the bank and sent a shower of arrows at us
but was shot down so fast, came no more but fell back and tried
to gain our rear and a despreate fight insued. They stood their
ground and faught until their leader Cordova was shot down[10]
and then retreated to the brush below us on the creek and set
up a howl like a lost dog and would never ralley anymore.

Their loss was thirty six dead and wounded including their
leader Cordova still on the ground. With but one man, Calvin
Turner, slightly wounded, the ball cuting the skin and som hair
from his temple, we soon dispached the wounded Indians and
turned our attention once more to the Mexicans. This time the
Mexicans did not form a circul for their platoons but came within
thirty yards of our imbankment and sent their platoons, about
fifty in nomber, one after another in full run to the edge of the
bank, fire and file to the left giveing place to another, all the
time in a run, always over shooting us, but we could see them.
Every platoon that fired thare would from five to ten be seen to
fall until thare was so many of them kild that the dead and
wounded obstructed their way, so that they could [not] run
so close, consequently, thare was fewer kild. Each charge kept
this up until about one oclock when they drew off, mounted

[10] Brown (*Indian Wars and Pioneers*, p. 66), who says he "watched the affair
closely although he was in another company," says Cordova was shot by John
Lowe. But A. J. Sowell (*Early Settlers and Indian Fighters of Southwest Texas*
[Austin: Ben C. Jones & Co., 1900], pp. 25, 422) says that Wilson Randle of Se-
guin killed Cordova. It could have been either of these two, as they were both in
Caldwell's group of volunteers.

their cavelray and sent them with the artilry out of sight on the flat, leaveing the infentry to hold us in position.

They had not been gone but a short time before we heared a furious canonading on the flat. It was then that Dawsons mas-[acre] was enacted. Dawson was in the open prairie and was makeing preperations to charge through the Mexican lines and try to gain Caldwells position when the Mexicans turned loose their artilry on them and was mowing them down like grain before a reaper. Dawson retreated to a small mot of mesquete trees which was literly tore into splinters by grape and canister and gun shot, killing over half of his men with no chance to fire a gun as the Mexicans kept out of rainge of their rifles. When the Mexicans thought they had kilt all but a few, the cavilry charg cam to finish up their work. Dawson raised a white flag in token of his serender and was instantly shot down. The rest [of] the men, seeing their leader shot down and the cavelry charg[ing] them, thought their time had come and stood still.

One man, Alsa Miller, who we left on a recruiting expedition and who d[i]d not return in time to join Caldwells Command but had fallen in with Dawson on the way, raised his white hand-kerchief on [his] gun stick. The stick was shot into splinters in his hand. He then fled for his horse but his horse was gone. By this time several balls [had] pierced his hat and cloaths. He then made for a horse that [was] tied close by. As he mounted he saw another man shot down trying to display a white flag.

By this time the Mexicans had completely serounded them and the work of death was going on. Miller, seeing a third man shot down holding a white flag, [det]ermined to make his escape or be kiled trying. He had nothing to loos in making the effort and all to gain if successfull, and turned his horses head eastward, that being the [di]rection to Seguin, bent low on his horse and made a desperate charge. Strange to say the Mexicans opened a gap in their lines for him to run through and as he passed the line he lost his hat. He says he believes it was shot off for as he passed they opened crossfire on him. He sed he suposed thare was a hundred shots fired at him before he was out of range of their guns.

When he had got clear he ventured to look back, and he saw eight or ten Mexicans in persuit. The horse he was ride[ing was] a large clumsy animel, a good saddle horse, but not fle[ete a]nd had received a wound. After passing the [line] he looked again [and] saw his persuers was gaining on him and at the same time he saw another horse at his heels with bridle and saddle on and a small mesquete limb draging to the bridle. The horse evidently had broak loose and had passed the lines close after him. He looked again and saw his persuers pressing him so close that the loose horse mad an efert to pass him. He felt his clumsy animel fast giving way from loss of blood and that his time was short, but just as the loose horse was opiset him, the thought struck him that if he was on that horse he might make his escape, strained every nerve and mad a leape from one horse to the other while both ware runing at top speede.

He settled himself in the saddle, bent forward, got the briddle, divested it of the mexquete limb and about this time he heard one of his persuers hollow and say, "Stop, Miller, and give up and you shant be hurt!" He thought the voyce was familer and on turning he saw Antonio Periz, the traitor, and one other in close persuit. They evedent[ly] had no fire armes or they could have shot him twenty times [b]ut they depended on takeing him alive by outruning him. When they saw him change horses they thought it a dowtful case but redoubling their efforts after hollowing, they seem[ed to g]ain on him. He said it was licket a brindle [for awhile and the] race seemed doubtful until I imageon he took in the situation at a glance and gave his horse his spurs and carried him a few [more] yards, shook him loose and he just touched a few of the [high] places that hapened to be in the next two miles and [whe]n his horse began to run leavel again, he ventured to l[oo]k back again but saw nothing of his persuers and stoped [to let] his horse blow a few seconds He traveled all that night and mad it to Seguin next morning bareheaded, in his shirt sleeves, and in the race he had lost one of his boots.

He told his story saying, "We dont know the fate of Caldwel

and his men. They may all have shared the fate of Dawson and his men."[11]

Thare was one other man, Gonzalvo Woods, mad his escape home to the Colorado Valley but the perticulars of which I never learned from himself so I shal not attempt to give them.[12] Dawson lost 32 killed, 15 taken prisners and 2 mad their escape.

After this terrable masacree the Mexicans mad another attact on our position with all their forces with threats and promaces but with about the same result except our men in this last charg had become more carless and dareing and 4 or 5 more received wounds. The second and last desperate charge they mad they wounded two more men but lost so many men, as our men had become so bold they crawled up on top of the bank and received the two last charges, that the officers could not make, hire nor perswaid them to make another charge.

[T]hey made several unsuccessful attempts and finely gave it up, drew off, and held a consultation and then sent in a flag of truce, asked leave to remove their dead and [w]ounded off the field which was granted, and an armistes [was] a[g]reed upon that hostiltes should scease until six oc[lock in the even]-ing. The squeeking nois of the wooden wheels of [carts comme]nced.

---

[11] Nance (*Attack and Counterattack*, p. 375) tells of Miller's escape thus: "The other escapee was, as we have already noted, Alsey S. Miller. He was pursued in his flight by Antonio Pérez and other renegade Mexicans, formerly of San Antonio. His mount was soon winded, but luckily he was able to seize Edward T. Manton's fine horse which had escaped from the grove and came galloping by at just the right time. With a better mount, Miller soon outdistanced his pursuers and arrived safe at Seguin—bare-headed, badly sunburned and with his horse covered with foam. This was the first news to arrive eastward from the battlefield."

[12] Sowell (*Early Settlers and Indian Fighters*, p. 817) gives this account of Gonzalvo Woods' escape: ". . . met Gonzalvo Woods, who made his escape from Dawson's Massacre, and was badly wounded. . . . a Mexican lancer dashed upon him with a leveled lance, and Woods caught it and gave such a quick, strong pull that it jerked the Mexican from his horse to the ground, and he wrenched the lance from his grasp and ran it through his body and pinned him to the earth, and then pulling it out, mounted the Mexican trooper's horse and made his escape, carrying the lance with him, which he still had, and which was very bloody." This lance is now in the Alamo Museum in San Antonio, having been placed there by the Woods family.

It was reported afterwords by the citizens ...[13] cart loads of wounded and lodged thim in the hospit[al] and thare was 12 or 15 wounded left on the field. They did not remove [any o]f their dead nor was they ever removed or burryed. The sun was [gone] behind the western horizen when the armistes was agreede upon.

Several of the boys whose horses had been broken loose by the falling limbs cut from the timber by the cannon balls that morning now went in serch of their horses. William Hesskew, Calvin Turner and John R. King soon found their horses and came back, leaveing Steven Jett and Simon Cockrel still in serch of theirs.

It seems that when Cordova was killed and his Indian allies was defeated by the guard that the Indians ran off down the creek carrying with them several wounded, som of which died whare they halted and set up such a howl. They afterword sculked around down thare in the timber until hostilities had sceased and the boys went in serch of their horses, discovered them and gave chase. Jett being the farthest down the creek they soon overtaken, kilt and scelped him. Several of them chased Cockrel so close and shooting him in the shoulder with a ball and two arrows, he had to take refuge by jumping in the creek whare it was very deep but crawled under a shelving bank where he could keep his nose out of the water and hid. The Indians he said stood on the bank over his head for several minuts watching for him to rise from the bottom of the creeke but gave it up and left. When the nois of their receding footsteps died away in the distance he emurged from his hideing place and mad his way to camp.

We had not yet learned the cause of the withdrawel of the Mexican cavelry and the heavy cannonading on the flat that evening and thare was vairious congectures concerning it. Som said it was a rouse to draw us out of our position, others said they undoubtly was fighting a conciderable company of recruits that was trying to gain [Ca]ldwells position. That was also my own opinion, and we was anxious to learn the truth [about] the

---

[13] Part of manuscript missing for which no information can be supplied.

squeeking nois of the carts. I placed out the guards and was sitting by the fire studdying over the events of the day when Henry McCulloch, Clem Hinds and Eli Hankens rode up to the [fire,] members of Hays spy company.

McCulloch says, "Jim, you leave the guard long enough to ride around with us while the guard is already stationed. We want you to pa[ss] us through and back."

"All right," says I, and turned to Cal[vin Tur]ner saying, "Take charge of the guard, Cal, until I return."

[H]e says, "All right, Jim, go ahead."

I saddled my horse, and we set out rideing to Wolls position. We discovered 15 or 20 dead Mexicans who had been carried thare wounded. Rideing on in the flat we come to Dawsons battle ground and the dead boddies almost in piles and could now realize the whole affaire. It was dark and we could not recognze any of the faces of the slain.

After rideing around a while and found [that] the Mexican army had scedadled and left us masters [of the] situation we went back to camp and reported our [discov]eries. I supose thare was a half dozen squads went [to bring] in the dead of Dawsons massacree, frying out greese [to make] lamps of their frying pans with the shirtsleeves [cut out to use] for wicks. The boddy of Jett was braught up [to the camp] and Wm. Hesskew taken charge of the boddy a[s they both had wor]ked on the same ranch togeather. Our w ... or and the men had satisfide their long-in ... tasted nothing sence early morn s ... silent slumber and nothing c ... pawing and snorting of the impatiant and ... horses.

The next morning at roll call it was asser[tained] that our loss was one killed, Jett, and eight wound[ed], Simmonds in lower part of bowells, Simon Cockrell in shoulder, Creed Tailor in shoulder, Roller Davis in arm, Jesse Zumalt in shoulder, John Law in thigh, Sam Callaghan through both hips, Calvin S. Turner slight temple. These all recovered except Callaghan. He was tak[en] to Seguin and in a few days died.

As soon as daylight appeared thare could be seen groops of men out examinin[g] the battle ground and amongst the rest was old Zekel Smith, our hero of Plum Creek. He found a wounded

Mexi[can] who had been shot in the mouth. The ball knocked out thr[ee] of his upper teeth and the same of his lower teeth and coming [out] on one side of his neckbone. The Mexican jabbered something to Smith and pointing to his mouth. The old man, not understanding him, taken him by one foot and ran near a hundred yards to the bank draging him over bushes, rocks and prick[ly] pares and turned him heels over head down the bluff, upset coffee pots, frying pans and lodging him in the fire but the man that was kooking his breakfast at the fire draged hi[m] out and talked strong of rideing the old man but was prevented.

The old man went round to another place and came down saying, "French, I braught you a pet, do you [want] him."

French says, "Father, you aught to be ashamed of yourself, treateing a human being in such a way."

The old man says, "He aint no human, he's a Mexican."

They sent [for] me. I talked with the wounded Mexican awhile. He said [he] was forsed to fight but he was shore he would never figh[t] Americans again. I gave him some coffee, he drank it and [asked for] a shuck and toback, mad a cigaret and smoket it. [I saw] him in San Antonio three years after and he knew me and said, "O, mucho amego, good friend." He said I saved his life.

The Mexicans lost in this fight 96 kilt dead on the ground and 16 wounded left on the ground. The Mexican citizens at San Antonio said thare was a hundred and twenty one braught in thare and of which twenty seven died of their wounds. After breakfast Caldwell called the men togeather in consultation and it was decided to follow Woll and finish cooking his goose and was makeing arangments to leave som men to bury the dead and take care of the wounded when Captain Jesse Billingsly rode into camp with 16 companions. After hearing the whole story concerning the battle and Dawsons massecree, he volenteered his servises and that of his men to stay and bury the dead and convey the wounded back to Seguin as Dawson and all his men ware his neighbors and we amediately set out in pursuit of Woll. Billingsly sent to San Antonio and precured tools and all nessaries for burrying the dead and conveyance for all the wounded except Callaghan. He had to be conveyed on a litter. He also procured medical aid for the wounded.

We expected to find Woll forted up in town but when we arived at that place Woll had scedadled, got farther and faster leaveing in disgust, and the most of the Mexican citizens had joined Woll in the fight and was afraid to stay and with Wolls consent and assistance they robed and pillaged the town. They too had left.

We learned this and renewed our energies in persuit. We soon saw by the goods and chattles scattered along the way with broaken carts that it had been a perfect flight or hurrying time. This was done by the greedy citizens, in their love of gain they had stolen more than they cou[ld ca]rry off. We marched on to the Madena and halted to refresh o[ur sel]ves and hungry horses that had not had a bite sence leaving Cibola two days and a half and two nights. While here resting [C]ol John H. Moor, Major Fields and Col. Mayfield arived with [a]bout 600 men. They halted also and commenced the same old game of wranggleing to see who should take command. They out [ta]lked Caldwell and out voted his men and gave the command [to] Col. Moor. I did not like the procedeings and told Caldwell as a goodly nomber of Caldwells men turned back from here and when we resumed our march I joined Hays Spy Company.

We over [ta]ken som families and learned from them that Woll was not [o]ver five miles a head of us, and Moor sent Hays on to scirmish with the enemy and hold them in check until the main force [co]uld come up, and about one hour by sun that evening we hove [in] sight of them som half mile a head of us, and Hays sent a runner back to Moor to double quick to his assistance. We mad a charge on their rear and found them badly scattered crossing the Hondo Creek. Their artilrey was in the rear and in this charge we captured four pieces of their cannon, two morters and two nine pounders, but we could not use them as they ware all emty and the amanition wagon was a head and we had not captured it. The rear guard, about 200 men, turned on us and a desprate fight insued. We faught them back and held

the 4 pieces of cannon till they gave way and retreeted back to
the creek when they were reinforst by the whole cavelry commanded by Seguin. They charged again, we still faught and beat
them back again but they rallyed and mad a furious charge. Seeing we was so out nombered and Moor not in sight, we gave them
ground and they retaken the cannon.

But we had held the cannon three quarters of an hour
ag[ainst] such odds expecting every moment Col. Moor to arive
with [the] main force. We drew off, having two men dangerously wounded, one man Arch Gipson shot in the eye bone glancing across his nose and Elonzo Perry, better known among old
Texians as Cattles Perry, badly wounded in the bowels. The Mex-
can loss was 33 dead and 13 wounded not taken off the battle
ground and it was reported by Col. Andrew Neill, one of the lawyers taken at San Antonio and released at Monterey by claiming
protection under the Inglish government and as not being taken
under arms was released, that thare was over forty wounded, several of which died on the retreat or it more resembled a flight
than a retreat.

When Col. Moor heared the firing ahead of him he had just
crossed a deepe wide ravine, and he ordered a retreat back to this
ravine, saying to his men, "Form in the hollow four deep and
every man to take one or two extra bullets in his mouth so as to be
convenant to reload."

He then rode up and down the line on top the bank, incourage-
ing his men, telling them to keepe cool and when the fight opened
to take good aim and we was shore of the victory. Thare he was
expecting to see Hays chased back to the main boddy and thare
we was fighting and holdeing the ground expecting every moment to see him with the main force charge in to the fight.

After remaining in his posision for a half hour and the fireing
ahead had sceased, Col. Moor emerged from his hideing place
and came up just as night was closeing in. We camped on one
side of the creek. The Mexicans halted on the other and built up
about one hundred fires out of dry mesquete logs and limbs and
silently took up the line of march. Their fires burned nearly al

night. We camp[ed on] the ground whare we had faught, and Moor ordered the men to [sleep] on their arms, holding their horses, and put out a double guard intending to attack the Mexicans soon after midnight when the moon would rise. Just after dark Henry McCulloch took two or three companies unbeknown to Hays and went round the head of a ravine to watch the manuvers of the enemy. He saw they ware kindling large fires and returned.

He went to Hays and asked him how the wounded men was gitting along. He said he did not know, that he had not seen them since dark.

"Whare are they," demanded Henry.

"I do not know that either," said Jack, "but supose they are in the hands of their friends."

"Thats a dam prety come off," said Henry, as he rose to go. "You have two wounded men in camp and dont know whare they are."

He searched and inquired until he found Gipson lying on a blanket by the root of a tree and his brother Jim sitting by him, and Perry was off to one side lying on a blanket and both begging for water. The only water was a pool near the mexican camp and they could git no one to venture thare.

Clem Hinds who had been out with Henry and had still continued with him in the serch for the wounded, heard their pitaful moans and cries for water, geathered up about a half dozen canteens and saying, "I will go if I git shot in the attemt!"

He was not gone long before he returned with watter, setting the canteens down by the wounded men, went to his mess fire to eat his supper. The Mexican fires war burning brightly, but thare was no nois.

About two hours after dark the ever watchful Hays thought the nois in the Mexican camp had hushed too soon and says, "Boys, that is something rotten in Denmark. That camp over thare is as still as death. Who will go with me to see whats in the wind."

Thare was about twe[nty] voices saying, "I'll go!"

Said he, "Dont all speak at once. I only want two men to go with me, more than that [wo]uld be dangerous."

"Well, then," said one, "you will have to [ch]oose for yourself."

Then sed he, "I will take Ice Jones and Jim Nichols."

We armed ourselves and set out. We crawle[d] cautiously through the brush in the bottom across the creek and keeped a good lookout for Mexican sentenels but saw none. We crawled up so we could see the fires and waited sometime, could see no one stiring. We examined all the fires and saw thare had been no cooking done. We knew then that it was a roose to detain us until they would git away.

Col. Neill said the way they traveled, Woll and his suit in front in a four horse ambulanch stolen out of the livery stable at San Antonio with a negro driver. Behind him was a file of soldiers, behind them ware the prisners—the judg, five lawyers, twenty fore jurymen and eight citizens and fiteen of Dawsons men—53 in all. Then came the infantry, behind them the cavelry, behind them the artilrey to bring up the rear.

We went back and reported the Mexicans gone. It created conciderable excitement, some cursing Moor in his hearing.

Others would hollow out, "Form in the hollow with bullets in your mouths," and all such taunts.

It certainly is true that if Moor had of double quicked, as Hays turned it, we could totaly demolished Wolls army and probbly not one would have mad his escape to tell the story, but instid thare of, he rode proudly and tryumphantly off with his 53 prisners. Or, had we not come in contact with Moor and his six hundred men, we could have, useing Caldwells fraze, coo[ked] Wolls goose.[14]

_____

[14] Many accounts have been written about this battle on the Hondo River, each different from the others. The story depends to a large degree upon which company the writer was in and which commander he served under. Mathew Caldwell was commanding on the Salado, but after John H. Moore and James S. Mayfield arrived with their groups of men there appear to have been conflicting commands. Captain Jack Hays' company was acting as scout ahead of the main body of Texans and, augmented with a few volunteers, seems to have been the only unit actually to make

Thare was but one thing that the writer blamed Caldwell with, that was in submiting himself and men to the command of Moor. He could have retained the command of his men as an independent company as did Hays.

Caldwells men, all but two, Ewing Cameron and Zeke Smith, decided not to follow Woll any farther as our horses was so jaded and hungry and ourselves wourn out. Next morning Caldwells outfit saddled up and set out. On our return, the two wounded men [were] in a Mexican cart drawn by a yoak of oxen which outfit had been abandoned by the Mexican citizens in their flight, with the cart bed filled half full of our blankets to make a soft bed for the wounded. We had mad but one days travel and camped on the Madena when Genl Summerville arived from Austin with one thousand men and a regular outfit of baggage, wagons, provision, etc. He said his orders was to follow Woll to the Reo Granda but not to cross.

A little explaination here might not be amiss. At the alarming news of the invadeing army when Woll entered and captured San Antonio, which flew like the wind and, of corce, reached Austin without delay, General Summerville, then General in Chief of the Malitia, was ordered to raise one thousand men and repair to San Antonio to repel the invesion.

The General sent out recruiting officer to beat up for volenteers but could not raise the required nomber. The Governor then ordered a draft on the malitia and while the officers ware prepairing their men and outfit for a three months campain, Caldwell with a handfull of men met and defeated the enemy and sent him on the run back home. And now after Woll was nearing the Reo Granda this a[rmy] was ready and on the march.

Wolls army was not intended as an invadeing army as reported but only to prevent the action of the court. Had the Mexi-

---

fighting contact with Woll's retreating army. When Hays charged the Mexican position at the cannon he was to have been backed up by Captain William M. Eastland with a group of picked mounted men, but instead Eastland was called back and Hays had to give up the cannon after holding it only a short time. The Texans thus lost their chance to overtake the Mexican forces. Generally it has been believed that disputes over who was to be in command were responsible for this failure.

can government sent an invadeing army suficient to have invaded even a potion of Texas and we had to wait the moovements at Austin, Caldwells men might have had the honor of defending the country or might have shared the fate of Fannin, Travis and Dawson and mad Thermopylae out of San Antonio.

After Caldwell examined Summervilles outfit he laughed and said, "As to the good you can do, you had as well turn back for you will never overtake Woll this side of the Reo Granda."

Summervill invited us all to join him. Two of our men joined the expedition, Ewing Cammern and Old Ezekel Smith. Evedently Cammeron and Smith had their plans metured before they started and that was to fillabuster on the other side. We will now follow Summerville. He taken the trail that Woll made and folled it to the Reo Granda, but when he arived thare he was informed that Woll had crossed over five days before.

Summerville hung around thare som weeks trying to learn wheather or not the government intended sending another army into Texas but could learn nothing reliable and mooved down and down until he arived at Rancho Davis. All this time Cammeron and Smith ware bussy at workeing on the minds of the soldiers. Summerville began to talk about returning. Cammeron thought now was his chance and tried to persuade the Gen'l to cross over with the whole force but to no efect, he then told the gen'l that he and a part of the men was going over anyway so Summerville mustered his command one morning and read his orders from the govrnme[nt] stateing that it was his intention to set out on his return.

The next morning while the men was in line Cammeron made them a gloing speech stateing to them how easy it would be to make a fortune in a few days and that it would only be retaliating as the Mexicans had done the very same thing which as they all knew, that they ware then on a campaign following Woll who had sacked San Antonio. He then called for volenteers to go accross with him. There was one or two entire companies and from ten to sixty from the other companies joined him.[15]

[15] Sowell (*Early Settlers and Indian Fighters*, p. 60) gives this account of the Sommervell Campaign: "In 1843, in retaliation for the invasion of Texas under

That was the starting point for the Mier prisners. Old Uncle Zeke drew a white bean and lived to return home. Cammeron drew a white bean and they said it was not fare and he drew another white bean but they shot him any way. That expedition has been detailed by fare mor able pens than mine so I will not attempt it.[16]

Summervill returned with all his men that would obey orders and was disbanded at Austin. Caldwell returned to Seguin and turned his men loos and every one went his way but for months a person could hardly hear anything else talked about but incidences in the battle of Salado and from the very outset intelligent men and close observers would differ in their statements about the same occurance but it has ever been so in all ages, but espelly so of those who has writen on these subjects years afterwords. They have so perverted the facts and writen so many abserdities that I hav been constrained to write this little book in self defence, not from memory alone but from notes taken at the time and place. For instance, one writer in narating some incidences in this battle Salado says one m[an] Creede Tailor while in camp here, leaveing the impresion that we had been in camp for a week or more, when we arived thare just about sundown and the enemy opened fire on us at sun up next morning, went down to the creek to w[ash] out his shirt and not having a chang in camp had to wait for it to dry. While doing so assended a pecan tree for the purpose of filling his pockets with pecans, quite early for pecans to be opening, and while thare was fired on from camp. He amediately decended and went to camp and demanded an explaintion. He was told that som Irish recruits who had just arived

---

Wall, an expedition started to Mexico under General Somerville. Captain Hays and his rangers were along, but the expedition went to pieces on the Rio Grande and most of the men came back. Five Captains, however, determined to go on in the invasion of Mexico if they could get men enough. Three hundred men came over to them. Among these were Big Foot Wallace, Sam Walker, and others of the rangers. The captains were William S. Fisher, Ewing Cameron, Eastland, Reese, and Pierson. After the separation they went down the river four miles and went into camp."

[16] Nichols refers to the execution of some of the men who split off from Somervell and were taken prisoner by the Mexicans when they attacked Mier. The Mexicans mixed black and white beans and forced their prisoners to draw lots; those who drew black beans were shot.

from Goliad had taken him for a Mexican spying out the camp and comenced this fucilade.[17]

Now the truth is thare was no recruts from Goliad ever arived. Creede Tailor was wounded early in this fight but recovered and still lives now on the head of Little Devils River and can be seen or writen to and will willingly answer all questions put to him concerning this fight.

Again, the same writer says Calvin Turner received a glancing shot in the head and fell. His brother William who was near, vainly trying to force a tiet ball down his gun, droped it, ran to him and assisted him to his feete and he soon recovered.[18] Now I will be compeled to reveil something that never would have been made public had not this statement been mad. I will state again that I was sergent of the guard and had charge and command of the guarde. Calvin and Bill was both on guard that day and we was stationed at and above the mouth of the lower ravine which Cordova was sent down and when Cordova and his band was discovered I ordered a charge and the men charged heroicly and a desprate fight insued. They was repeled but soon rallyed and come again, and again they give back and undertook to scale over the bank, but we met them and repulsed them again.

In this charge Cordova was kiled and his Boluxie Indians would rally no more. Calvin Turner was wounded in the first charge. I was by his side and he neither fell nor flinched from his gallient fighting. Cal was a brave man. When we saw that the Indians would rally no more we all returned to our position but

[17] Nichols is referring to A. J. Sowell who in *Rangers and Pioneers of Texas*, p. 213, wrote: "While encamped here, Creed Taylor went down to the creek, a short distance below the camp, for the purpose of washing out his shirt, and not having a change in camp, had to wait for it to dry. While doing so he ascended a pecan tree for the purpose of filling his pockets with pecans, but as soon as he arose above the level of the prairie, was fired at from camp, the balls cutting the limbs around him. He hastened down, donned his half dry shirt, and proceeding to camp, demanded an explanation, and was told that some Irish recruits from Goliad, who had just arrived, had taken him for a Mexican spying out the camp, and commenced the fusilade upon him."

[18] "Calvin Turner received a glancing shot in the head and fell; his brother, William, who was near, vainly endeavoring to force a tight ball down his rifle, dropped it and ran to him, and assisted him to regain his feet, and he soon recovered" (Sowell, *ibid.*, pp. 216–217).

still kept a close look out for the Indians to attact us again.

When all had settled down again and all reloaded, Calvin ses to me, "I wonder whare Brother Bill is. I haven't seen him since you first ordered a charge."

I says, "I have not seen him neither. He may be kilt or wounded som whare!"

Cal says, "Lets git some water, I am auful thirsty and then I will look him up."

We started down to the creek and found Bill couched down behind a large pecan tree. Cal says, "Bill, are you wounded."

He says, "No!" and whined out in a half cry, "I got my gun choaked and I dident think it worth while for me to stand out thare and be shot at when I couldent shoot back."

Cal taken his gun, pushed the ball down, handed it to him and told him to take it and go to fighting like a man. But the next charge the Mexicans made, Billy was no whare to be seen.

Now, reader, you might think the reason I write this is that Bill is dead and Cal is still liveing but to the reverse. Calvin died in 1862 and Bill is still liveing or was a few months ago. He lives near old Camp San Saba.

After Miller entered Seguin next morning after the battle and told his story and could give no account of the fate of Caldwell and his men, John[19] and Milford decided to mount their horses and set out amediately for the scene of action and haveing a lot of cooked beef on hand and thinking the most of the soldiers had past and heard the fireing of the cannon distinctly the day before from the time the sun rose, felt some uneasyness as to their fate. They mounted their horses and set out but on nearing the battle ground met Captain Billingsly and his men with the wounded soldiers.

Learning the perticulars of the battle and that Caldwell was in pursuit of Woll, the boys turned back to assist them in forwarding the wounded. When they arived the wounded ware all taken to Johns house except one Callaghan. He wanted to be alone. He was carried to an emty house and cared for until he died which was in a few days after his arivel.

[19] This was John Nichols, an older brother of James W. Nichols.

John and his wife[20] acted the good Semeritan in ministering to
the wants of the wounded in washing cloths and bandages, dressing wounds and prepareing something for them to eat. Thare was
seven of them and it kept them buisy. Of course, they had help
from others in the town but it kept all hands buisy and they slept
none that night from the moans and groans and raveing of the
sufferers.

In a few days four of them was carried by their friend and relatives to their homes, Jesse Zumalt, John Law, Creed Tailor and
Sol Simononds. Cockrel and Davis remained sometime longer but
they all recovered. In a few days John and his wife willingly sub-
mited to a repetition of the same kind of trouble. Our two men
wounded at the Hondo fight, Gipson and Perry, was taken thare
but Gipson remained but a short time as his brother Jim was with
him and soon Arch was able to be carried home but Perry remain[ed] several weeks but both recovered.

Now let me stop right here and say that this old vetran lady is
still living but destitute of any means of makeing a living and
through age and infirmity has had to throw herself on the charity
of her friends and relatives for suport and let me say again that it
is a burneing shame upon our legislatures to neglect to provide
for the suport of such heroic women who has given themselves
out in the servis of their country. It was such that helped to cut
the brush and blaze the way and smooth down the rough places
in the path where civilization was marching stedily on.

I say, give them a pension suficient for their suport and settle
their sorrows and brighten their furrowed cheeks and make them
forget their cares in their declining years. Thare are many wom-
en who is less deserving and who is young and vogrous but is
playing second fiddle to som old vetren gentlemen and injoying
his pension. Now I say again, pension these old widowes who has
no means of suport except through their friends and relatives.

Now if I was writeing a history of all battles in Texas I should
give a morre detailed account of battles in which many heroi

20 Polly Day Nichols, sister of Milford Day, who married John Nichols in 183
(see Chapter II). At the time Jim Nichols wrote this book John Nichols was dead.

deeds of valor and wharein many brave and good men and officers ware engag such as Ed Burleson, Mayfield, Summerville, Houston, Rusk, Ford, Fields, Baylor, Bowie, Tumbleston, Grumlles, Hysmith, Byrd, Fryer, Moor and others too tedious to mention of lesser lights, but not haveing served under or with but few of them I shal leave them out. I cannot write them all up in as small a work as I contemplate writeing though as Ed Burleson and my father was raised togeather from boyhood and was always fast friends I will relate one circumstance. Father loved his dram and sometimes he would git woozy. On one occaision of this kind when Father had about two sheets in the wind and another fluttering, a stranger to Father steped up to him and says, "Mister, what might you name be."

Father says, "It might be John Tyler, John Smith or John Jones but it aint either. Sir, my name is rugged and tough and if thats not enough I could give you the rest but it might be too rough, for hear," showing his left fist, "is the mallet of death hung on the crank of independance." The man turned of.

Ed Burleson had been nominated for the legeslature and being a large croud presant they are discusing the merits and demerites of the candidates when a man, Henry Smith, staggered up to Father and says, "Uncle Rugged, who are you going to vote for."

Father says, "I am going to vote for Ed Burleson if I am able to git to the poles."

Smith hung down his head and repeated, "Ed Burleson, a common bear hunter. Why" turning up his eyes to Father, "he had not got sence enough to set a goose in a hay mound."

Just as he said "mound" Father turned the crank and away flew the mallet. O, reader, about ten steps from thare would have been seen a man gitting up holding in both hands a broken jawbone. He was just in the right fix to use gruel for the next five or six weeks. Smith went to hunt a doctor and Father went on with his drinking.

After my return from the Woll campaign everything seemed quiet. The Indian raids was few and fare between and thare being

"Father turned the crank"

no raingeing companies nor none neaded and on such ocaisions
I would run my wagon so I hitched my team and set out for Port
Lavaca. At Gonzales I taken on a load of hides, and the third day
out late in the evening I looked ahead of me and thought I saw a
women a foot but she was soon hid from my sight by a bend in the
road and I saw her no mor. I was aimeing for a creek ahead of me
to pitch my camp, and I arived at the creek, watered my team,
filed my bag and drove out to the edge of the prairie, and thare I
noticed a woman sitting by the root of a tree. I pulled out on the
other side of the road, stoped, turned out my team, carried up
som wood, started a fire and taken my grub box out and was going to prepare supper and had not noticed the woman come up to
me until she spoke saying, "I will git supper for you if you are
willing."

When she spoke I knew her voice. I says, "In the name of big
Peter, what are you doing here."

She ses, "I have left my old man and am going back to my people." I knew whare her people lived and it was a long trip she
had started.

She had nothing but an old fashened bandanner silk handkerchief tied up full of her best cloaths. After supper I asked her several questions as to how she expect to pay her way over the Gulf,
etc. and she said she was going to work her pasage over. She
traveled with me the rest of the way down.

When we arived thare was a scooner ready to sail. She bid me
fairwell, thanking me for my kindness, and entered the boat, and
I loaded my wagon and started out. It was then near sundown,
and I was near two miles on my way but had about three mor to
make to git water and grass. I looked back and saw her comeing
in a trot and she waved her bundle and I stoped, thinking maybe
she has forgoten something. She came up and said the captain
would not take her in to worke her passage. "And now," said she,
"I want to go back home with you."

I taken her back home and her and her husband lived togeather untill they raised a large family of children and he died.
I withhold her name as she is still lieving and respected.

CHAPTER IX

Hays Celebrated Rangeing Company. A Trip to Eastern Texas. Gitting Married. An Old Churn. A Three Dollar Colt. H. E. McCulloch Raises a Company. The Mexican War. Treed by Haverlieners. A Trip to Monterey. The Maid of Monterey.

❦ IN THE SPRING of 1843 the Comanche Indians became very troublesom in the west especially around San Antonio. John C. Hays aplied to the authorities at Austin and precured an order to raise a company of mounted rangers for twelve months servis,[1] and Calvin Turner, Joe Williams, John Rogers, William Deadman, James Roberts, and myself joined him.

We was stationed at the old mission below San Antonio. W. A. "Big Foot" Wallace was elected First Lieutenant and Ad Gelispi, Second, and we neaded no more officers. These with the Captain was to lead all scouts, and I was chosen trailer. We kept out scouts

[1] "An Act To Authorize the President To Accept the Services of One Company of Mounted Men To Act as Spies on the Southwestern Frontier. *Section 1.* Be it enacted by the Senate and House of Representatives of the Republic of Texas in Congress Assembled, That the President be, and he is hereby authorized to accept the services of one compnay of mounted men, to act as spies on the Southwestern Frontier, until the provisions of an act, entitled 'an act to provide for the protection of the Western and South Western frontier and for other purposes,' can be carried into effect. *Section 2.* Be it futher enacted, That the sum of five hundred dollars be and is hereby appropriated to carry out the provisions of this bill. *Section 3.* Be it further enacted, That this act take effect from and after its passage. Approved, 1 January 1843" (H. P. N. Gammel, *Laws of the Republic of Texas*, II, 865).

"Joint Resolution for the Relief of Captain John C. Hays, and the Company under His Command: Be it resolved by the Senate and House of Representatives of the Republic of Texas in Congress assembled, That the sum of six thousand four hundred and fifty dollars, be, and the same is hereby appropriated for the payment of Captain John C. Hays, with the company under his command, and the liabilities that have been created for the support of said company, while employed in the protection of the South-Western frontier, during the year one thousand eight hundred and forty three. Be it further resolved, That the Treasurer of the Republic be and he is hereby authorized to pay the six thousand four hundred and fifty dollars, as appropriated by this Resolution, to Captain John C. Hays, who is hereby authorized to receive the same and render his account of disbursements to the proper Department of the government. *Section 3.* Be it further resolved, that this resolution shall take effect from and after its passage. Approved, December 19, 1843" (*ibid.*, II, 915).

all the time, when one would come in another would go out, and those not on a scout ware every day practising horsemanship and marksmanship. We put up a post about the size of a common man, then put up another about 40 yards farther on. We would run our horses full speed and discharge our rifles at the first post, draw our pistles and fire at the second. At first thare was some wild shooting but we had not practised two months until thare was not many men that would not put his balls in the center of the posts.

Then we drew a ring about the size of a mans head and soon every man could put both his balls in the circul. We would practics this awhile, then try rideing like the Comanche Indians. After practisng for three or four months we became so purfect that we would run our horses half or full speede and pick up a hat, a coat, a blanket, or rope, or even a silver dollar, stand up in the saddle, throw ourselves on the side of our horses with only a foot and a hand to be seen, and shoot our pistols under the horses neck, rise up and reverse, etc.[2]

At one time being up in town at some pony races Calvin Turner and myself offered to bet ten dollars that either of our horses could beat any saddle horse in town, and we would ride standing in the saddle. We could not git a bet and in the evening him and I ran our horses through the track about half speed standing in the saddle. We had just been out practising and went into camp when som of the boys discover a man rideing at a breakneck gate comeing directly towards us.

On ariveing he says, "Indians, boys!"

He said thare was 30 or 40 Indians with near 50 head of horses, and we ware soon in our saddles, and leaveing a small guard in camp we started.

Hays says, "Jim, take two or three men and go ahead and find the trail."

I taken Joe Williams, Wallace, and Cal Turner, and we soon struck the trail and could easily follow it. They turned west and

[2] Wilbarger (*Indian Depredations in Texas*, pp. 290–295) gives an account of the famous "Riding Match" between Rangers and Comanches held near San Antonio in 1843, which was probably a result of this training.

crossed the Madina whare Castroville now stands. We could gallop on the trail and soon found it very fresh. We assended a ridge, espied them, and droped back out of sight, and motioned Hays to double quick which he did, and we again assended the hill and I pointed to the Indians. We waited until they went behind a point of timber and Hays ordered a charge, and charged up within two hundred yards of them before they discovered us. They halted for a moment as though they was going to fight us, but when they saw our nomber they wheeled their horses and done their best runing. We had a runing fight for about four miles when they left their horses and took to the rough ceder mountain on foot.

We kilt six in the run and at the edg of the break we kilt three more, and how many was wounded we never knew. We recaptured all the horses and all their equipments, and rounded up all the horses and their accutrements and traveled til dark gitting to a creek whare we could git watter. The Indians followed us and mad two or three unsuccessful attempts to stampede our horses, but we had them too strongly guarded. We arived back the next day and delivered the stolen horses to their owners.

The next morning Hays says, "Boys, keepe up your practicen shooting horseback. It beats the Indians at their own game."

That was the last fight I was in while I belonged to Hays company. A weeke or two after this I was up in town and got a letter from a man in Walker County who had mooved from Seguin owing me near a hundred dollars. The letter stated that he would pay off the note in property if I would go after it, and I decided to go. I told Captain Hays about it and he says, "Jim, it will be mighty hard to do without you, you and Cal are two of the best horsemen and marksman in the company. Can't you wait until the turm of servis is out."

I says, "Captain, now is the time."

I got a man, Kit Acklin, to take my place and was soon on my way to Walker County accompened by Brother Solmon and his wife, John Sowell and his wife[3] going out thare on a visit. On ariveing I found my man and received som good promaces but nothing else.   [3] This was Jim Nichols' sister Elizabeth.

John C. Hays Rangeing Company

While thare I wood and won and married the daughter of Reverend George Danill who had lived in Gonzales County som years, and after the Woll campaign mooved to Walker County. After I married I set in to work with old Billie Winters making chiers, looms, reels, etc. The next spring I bought som cows and was gitting plenty of milk. My wife wanted a churn and thare was no such a thing to be baught in the country them days and I concluded to make one. I went to the woods and found an old mulberry tree that perhaps had been dead for a hundred years. The bark and sap had all rotted off many years before. I cut it down, taken the log and mad a churn and when we use a churn now we use that one. It has never needed any repares and is apearently as sound and as good as it was 43 years ago.[4] I learned my trade well and in the fall of '44 as Brother Solomon and Brother-in-law John Sowell was preparing to return I conclude to go with them. I baught the tooles and all the unfinished work giveing 19 head of cattle. Winters was to deliver all at Seguin and assist me two months in erecting a shop and gitting the tools up in order.[5]

When the two months was up I had a good suply of furniture on hand and concluded to try the San Antonio market. I hired John Sowell to carry a load for me and we arived thare in the evening but in time to sell out. We went in to a wagon yard to

[4] The story of this churn was told to this editor by several members of the Nichols family before they knew of the account in Jim Nichols' journal.

[5] This must have been the same William Carvin (Billy) Winters who settled in Hays County sometime between 1846 and 1850. Williedell Schawe, in *Wimberley's Legacy* (San Antonio: Naylor Co., 1963), pp. 6–10, speaks of him as being the first settler of Wimberley.

William Carvin Winters and his brother John came to Texas from Tennessee in 1832 and settled in Walker County. Billy Winters went back to Tennessee to bring his family to Texas in 1834 and returned with his mother and father, his wife and children, and eleven brothers and sisters. They were living in Walker County in 1836, and James, John, and William all fought at San Jacinto, William being severely wounded. Sometime between 1845 and 1850 Billy Winters located in Hays County. By 1853 his house on Cypress Creek was finished and his family was with him there. At that time he and James Montgomery bought a thirty-four-acre tract of land at Cypress Creek Crossing and established a sawmill, known then as Winters' Mill, now as Wimberley. Winters died in 1864 at fifty-five years of age; his descendants still live in the area. It was probably the trip with Jim Nichols to Seguin in 1844 that prompted Winters to move his family to this area and establish his sawmill on Cypress Creek.

:amp, and after supper we concluded to take a stroll in town and
went round a while.

John says, "Lets hunt a saloon, take a drink and go back."

Directly we came to the Bullshead that was a saloon and gam-
bling house.[6] After takeing a drink we stood round watching
them gamble. Thare was from fifty to a hundred men and women
playing at every kind of a game then known. We was standing
near a montie table and thare was a man sitting at the table who
had lost his last dollar.

He turned to John and said, "Loan me a dollar five minuts."

John handed him the money and he bet and lost.

He says, "Loan me two dollars more. I know I can beat the dam
game."

He bet that and lost and I whispered to John and told him not
to let him have any more.

I says, "He would lose a bushel if he had it."

John turned and we walked off and next morning the same
man came round in the same yard and John knew him and says,
"Well, old pard, how did you come out last night with Mr.
Montie."

"Montie, hell," says he. "I lost an even hundred dollars and
then borrowed som from another man and lost that."

John says, 'Yes, I am the man you borred from."

"The hell you are," says he. "Well, how mutch did I borrow."

"Three dollars," says John.

He says, "Well, my friend, all I have left in this world is that
mare and yearling colt, and if you will take the colt for the three
dollars I will give the stable man my saddle and leave this dam
town barebacked."

John taken the colt and neither of us ever saw the man afterwords. We taken the colt home and it worried throug the winter
without attention, and the next spring John sold his colt to a

⁶ Frank H. Bushick, in *Glamorous Days* (San Antonio: Naylor Co., 1934), p.
108, gives the following description: "The old Bull's Head on Market Street was one
of the most notorious of the early day joints. Robberies and tragedies were not the in-
frequent outgrowth of the high and reckless play. That's the place they used to
sweep out the human hair and eyes the next morning after the night before." Most
stories about San Antonio of this period give highly graphic accounts of the "Bull's
Head."

negro for ten dollars. That fall I traded an old steer for the colt rated at fifteen dollars, and the next summer I broak him to ride.

He was a natural pacer, could go no other gait. He would pace when grazeing on the range, and I would a bet all I was worth that no man could git on him and whip or spur him out of a pace. I thought a great deal of him. Them days a man could buy a common saddle pony for ten or fifteen dollars, and I had several offers for him from 20 to fifty dollars, but I did not part with him.

Bill Clark was keeping a livery stable in Seguin and had mad me several offers. One day, said he, "Will you take sixty dollars for Stilts."

I says, "No."

"Will you take seventy."

I says, "No."

He says, "I have been studying for a week how to cheat you out of Stilts."

I says, "Well, I can tell you a plan that will work."

"Whats that," said he.

Thinking to bluff him off, "You can cheat me out of Stilts by giveing me one hundred dollars cash in hand before you take him."

He says, "I would play hell cheateing you that way."

I says, "Well, good by old pal," and started to mount.

He says, "Well, hold on. Its a trade."

He pade me the money and loned me a horse to ride home and Clark kept him over a year training him all the time to pace fast and over rough ground. One day thare came a man, Loui Thompson, a drummer from New Orleans, and put his team up with Clark, went round in town showing his samples. That evening he saw Clark exerciseing his horse and stood and looked perfectly amazed at the performance of the horse. In a day or two Thompson asked Clark if he would trade his horse.

"No, he suits me," said Clark.

He had been thare a week and one day he says to Clark, "I will give you choice of my horses for yours."

One of his horses was worth a hundred dollars. Clark says

"That is no inducement." He says, "How mutch money will you take for him." Clark did not want to part with his horse and thought he would bluff him off at the start and says, "I will take two hundred and fifty dollars for him," thinking the man would not think of giveing that amount for one horse.

Thompson says, "Here is your money," pulling out a roll of bills, "and the horse is mine."

Clark looked so foolish and felt more so, but the man counted out the money, tied a rope around the horses neck and drove off, and Clark cursed himself for a week afterwards.

Thompson taken the horse to New Orleans, had him trained, and made a bet of five hundred dollars that he could pace over ten whiskey barrels placed in a row a certin distance apart and never touch a barrel or brake his pace. He won the bet and then sold him at auction on the street for twenty one hundred and fifty one dollars and he was taken to England, Thompson told me this a year or two afterwords, away went that three dollar colt accross the deep waters.

I worked at my trade for about two years without having to do any milatary duty and in that time thare was no incident occured worth recording. In 1845 the Republic of Texas died and was burried in the anexation to the United States and was riserected in the shape of the State of Texas. Now the Fedral government was bound to protect us, as one of the compact and sent men and means for that purpose, but in 1846 the two nations, Mexico and the United States, got to wrangleing, over the result of anexation and war was declared and most of the troops had to leave Texas and go to Mexico and Texas had to raise troop to protect her own fronteer though at the expence of the Fedral government. H. E. McCulloch raised a company for three months servis. We was stationed whare San Marcos town now stands[7] and Brother John and Alsa Miller taken the contract to furnish corn and beef

[7] Dudley R. Dobie in his *A Brief History of Hays County and San Marcos, Texas* (San Marcos: n.p., 1948), p. 16 states: ". . . served as members of Captain Jack Hays Company of Rangers who were stationed where the United States Fish Cultural Station is now located. The ranger force was under the command of Captain Henry E. McCulloch."

for the turm. We had no inguagements with either Indians or
Mexicans, and we done very little good except to overawe and
keep back the Indians, but in that, no doubt, we done some good
as thare was not a single raid mad by Indians, while in this servis.
The Mexican War was now a reality as we knew by the government of the United States ishueing orders to every state for a
certain coto of men. Henry McCulloch received an order to raise
a full company for twelve month servis and when his three
months turm was out he beet up for volenteers for his next turm.

So in October the 7th myself, Solomon Nichols, John and Asa
Sowell, Milford Day, Simon Cockrel, Hardin Turner, and John
D. Pickens from Seguin joined him.[8] We was to furnish our own
clothing, horses, and arms, and the government furnished the rest
and we ware to receive thirty dollars pr month. That looked like
buisness.

We ware stationed at the same place. As Andrew Linzy who
owned the land layed of the town[9] soon after and nearly all of us
baught lots, built houses, and mooved our families thare, we remained thare through the winter. Thare was ten or a dozen companies raised along the fronteer on this order and was mustered
into the servis as fronteer raingers but subject to orders from the
War Department.

In the spring, the 2nd of March, an order was ishued to Gen'l
How then commanding that department to inspect all the troops
on the fronteer and such as ware well armed and well mounted he
should send on to Mexico and those that ware not armed and
equped as the law directs should remain at the posts. Our company was inspected first and thare was but few that was permited

[8] The National Archives, Washington, D.C. (Microcopy 278, Roll 12) shows the
following service record for James W. Nichols: "James W. Nichols, Corporal, age
25. Capt. H. E. McCulloch's Company. Colonel P. H. Bell's Regiment. Enrolled October 22, 1846 at San Marcos. Mustered out October 21, 1847 at Austin. Value of
horse—$50.00. Value of horse equipments—$15.00."

[9] Dudley R. Dobie (*Brief History of Hays County*, p. 19) says: "Gen. Edward
Burleson, Wm. Lindsey, and Dr. Eli T. Merriman entered into a joint ownership of
a 640 acre tract of land derived from the Veramendi Grant, and proceeded to lay
out the original town of San Marcos. These owners partitioned the lots among themselves after reserving some for public use."

to remain at the post. We was ordered to San Antonio to await orders. He went on inspecting and soon all of the troops arived, and were orgenized into a battalion, Tom I. Smith in command as Major,[10] and we set out on the march for Tailors army then at Monterey, Mexico. We marched by the way of San Petricio,[11] Kings Ranch, and on to Los Almos Wells and thar we found watter and grass and went into camp about noon.

Late that evening I concluded to try my luck for som fresh meat, a turky, rabbit, or squirrel as thare was an emence brake of mesquite, pears, and cheperal not fare off and I wended my way thither. I had not proceded fare into this brake before I espied a large heard of haverliners, a specia of musk hog, quietly feeding and I concluded to kill one and try his meat, having heard it said their meat was exclent to eat.

I fired at one wounding him severly and he fell and set up a horse squeel or howl, then the whole gang rallied around it and tore it litterly into mints bits.

While this was going on I was reloading my gun. When they ware through tearing the dead one to pieces they began searching around for the cause. I steped a few steps farther towards them in order to git a fair view for another shot and when I moved they espied me and came towards me in a full run poping their teeth, their haire turned the rong way, makeing a turable grunting, squeeling, or howling nois. It was fearful in the extream and I took refuge in a large mesquit tree but droped my gun at the root of the tree as I could not clime with it but droped it and ran up the tree like a squirrel.

By this time the sun had set and suposeing the animils would leave me soon I composed myself. But they kept up their boo-hooing nois and kept rallying and incircleing the tree until it seemed like they had increased to thousands and I could see gangs

---

[10] "Major Thomas I. Smith's battalion was short-lived, serving for April and May, 1847" (House Executive Document No. 24, Thirty-first Congress, First Session, page 22g).

[11] The town of San Patricio, on the north bank of the Nueces River in south-western San Patricio County, was the county seat at the time of the United States-Mexican War .

still comeing in every direction. I hollowed several times as loud as I could but seemed to be out of hearing of the camp.

I then concluded to await their hogships pleasure in leaveing me and placed myself in the fork of the tree watching their manuvers until several of them commenced naughing at the tree about a foot above the ground. They cut away a while then steped back looking up as mutch as to say, "We'll git you yet." I says, "I think you are left now," thinking they would give it up soon, as the tree whare they ware cutting was at least 16 or 18 inches through. But they cut away awhile and then steped back and looked up at me and about the same nomber took their places. I says, "Well, thats a new wrinkle," and it was astonishing to see how fast they would cut with their sharp teeth cutting out chips as large as a dime. I sit still until the third relief went on and I yelled, "For Gods sake."

At least they heard me at camp. It was then dark and they suposed I was lost and answered me to let me know which way camp was but I kept up such a yelling and bauling som of the boys started to me. They come within seventy or eighty yards and hollowed. I answered and informed them of my situation. They returned to camp and about twenty of the boys saddled their horses and came to relieve me.

Thare was one or two blankets spread at nearly every fire and men ware playing card, throwing dice, som cooking supper, som loling on their pallets. The chapperal was so thick the boys had to ride round on the opposit side to git an open place to git to me, gitting me and the haverlines between them and the camp and comcenced a turiable fucilade on them, all fireing one after the other in quick succession. Such a continious fireing gave them a scare and perhaps a thousand of them in a breast struck the camp, ran through, brakeing a great many horses loose, and scattering fire, cooking utentials, men, blankets, cards, and everything in their way. When we arived at camp I never saw men in such an excitement in my life. If the whole Comanche tribe had run through the camp it would not have created a greater excitement.

I went back to the tree next morning to git my gun and hat which I could not find that night and was surprised to see the tree naughed two thirds down. They could and would have fell the tree in two hours more if let alone.

We marched from thare to Rancho Davis[12] on the Reo Granda and while thare received news that our servises war not needed in Mexico. In a few days, however, we received a dispatch for us to hurry on. We crossd over and marched to Mier. We went into camp thare. The dispatches ware so unreliable, first one would come stateing our servises was not needed, then another for us to hurry up. Major Smith concluded to send dispatches direct to Gen'l Tailor and learn the facts in the case.

One morning we was ordered into line for roll call and while in line Smith made us a speech stateing his intention and said he, "It is a dangerous rout as the road is infested by bands of gurillies, free booters and now, boys, you may have som hard fighting or tall running to do, and I want twenty men and a liutenant to command them and I want them all to have good horses and if I cant git volenteers I will have to make a detail. Now, who will volenteer to go. All that will, let them step six paces to the front."

Thare was a pause for perhaps a minute, and I steped out. I stood alone a while and five or six more steped out. After another pause Smith began to talk about makeing a detail and thare was soon twenty in line.

Now said he, "One more and their will be the nomber."

One more came and no officer except myself and I was but a corporal.

Smith says, "Thare is fiteen lieutenants and none will volenteer. Well, men, choose you a leader," and all the men but three hollowed out, "Nichols. He was the first man out, and I know he will do."

The dispatches ware mad out and given to a trusty Mexican courier and guide and he wrote out a Lieutenants commision,

---

[12] W. H. Chatfield, in *The Twin Cities of the Border—Brownsville, Texas, and Matamoros, Mexico* (New Orleans: Privately printed, 1893), p. 43, says: "H. Clay Davis was first American settler in what is now Rio Grande City, settling there in 1846. . . . The place is still known as Davis' Ranch or Rancho Davis by most of the Mexican population. While travelling to Rio Grande City from Brownsville, the compiler was told of this peculiarity, and when two Mexicans got into the stage at San Miguel and were asked by the compiler's informant where they were going replied, 'Rancho Davis'!"

handed it to me, and we was off on a dangerous road—330 miles.

All went on well until the third evening out. We discovered a band of som thirty gurillies traveling paralel with us but near a mile distant. They ware sometimes in sight then out of sight all evening. The Mexican courier said they ware watching for a favorable opperunity to attack us or waiteing until night to stampede our horses and attact us. About sunset we halted, eat supper, mounted again, rode rappidly five or six miles, left the road some two miles, found good grass, and camped, put out one guard at a time, and the rest slept. In this way we dodged them as we could see their sighn next day all along the road.

We traveled on without molestation though we could see bands of these gurillies every day. One day we came upon the smoke-ing, smoldering remains of a wagon train where 80 wagons had been burned. The gurilles had attacted the train, kill all the teamsters, robed, and burned the wagons and the boddies of the teamsters had been burned with the wagons. This had been done not more than 24 hours before we passed. One day we saw a band of these gurillies about twenty in nomber crossing the road ahead of us. We charged them but they out run us and got away.

We arived at Liveoak Spring[13] whare Gen'l Tailor was camped delivered the dispatches, and went into camp. Next morning was

---

[13] Other accounts give the name for this location as Walnut Springs.

drill day with one ridgment. While we ware eating breakfast a big fat man rode up to whare they ware drilling and sat lazily on his horse watching them drill.

I says, "I will bet ten dollars I know that man."

"Who is it," says one.

I said, "That is judg Quitman. I have seen him in Texas."

After breakfast I steped accross the branch to whare he was and was convinced and mad myself known to him. I told him whare and when I had seen him in San Augustine ten years before. After talking awhile he says, "There is a grand curiosty in town three mile from here, and I am going thare this evening. I would like to have your company."

"What is the curiosity," said I.

"It is nothing but a garden," said he, "though I want you to see it. Will you go."

I says, "Certainly I will."

After dinner we set out and arived at the garden and a grand curiosity it was which I will try to discribe farther on. We bruised round town and he taken a great deal of paines showing me over the differant potions of the battle ground, potions of town which they would take and hold before storming another. We remained til late, and, with a promace that I would acompany him the next day, we parted.

He saying, "I want to show you through the Bishops Pallace tomorrow."

Next morning I got permission and taken all of my men with me. After showing me through the Bishops Pallace, and whare Gelispi fell and how that place was stormed, he went his way and we went to the garden.

The war was now about to come to a close. Despatches was sent to our command to return to Texas, but we was still retained. We remained in Monterey som two months before we was permited to return.

While thare I become a frequent visitor to Aristas Gardin. General Arista was a general in the Mexican army and received a wound at the battle of Buenavista which caused his death leaveing his emence state worth three millions to his wife, who had been blind over twenty years, and a single daughter. This gardin is the most beautiful arainged place I ever saw, a flower gardin with every known flower, shrub, and fruit that grows in a southern climate with a beautiful arainged bathing pool in the center. When I was thare it was frequented dayly by all the officers of the army.[14]

About ten days after my arivel the citizens gave the officers a ball or fandango. Thare was none invited but commissioned officers, and this young senorita, Selavia Arista,[15] was thare and her dress and jylery was veriously estemated at about 5,000 to 25,000 dollars. I had made her acquaintance a few days before, and as I could speake the Spanish language well, she seemed to look to me for protection and I had to interduce her at least fifty times that night. She was saught after and admired by many a young officer of Tailors army.

She was the noted senorita, the Maid of Monterey. She was the one that acted the charitable part to the wounded soldiers that caused David Cule, the little Irishman, who was wounded thare to compose the song known as "The Maid of Monterey."[16] She dressed herself in peon or servent cloaths and went ministering among the wounded soldiers. I will here insert the song.

[14] John R. Kenly (*Memoirs of a Maryland Volunteer* [Philadelphia: J. B. Lippincott, 1873], pp. 158–159) wrote: "I also visited the pride of the town, the palace of General Arista, a very wealthy citizen of Monterey. Our wounded filled its corridors and marble-paved halls, around whose cots heavy curtins, mirrors, vases, paintings, etc. were hanging and arranged in careless profusion. The gardens and baths were fitted up in luxurious style, and the Orange and the pomegranate mingled their perfume with the sweet rose of our own dear land. All was attractive, nay, enchanting."

[15] General Cadmus M. Wilcox (*History of the Mexican War* [Washington, D.C., Church News Publishing Co., 1892], p. 100) wrote: "One young girl, rich, beautiful and of distinguished lineage, Senorita Zozaya, compared by native authors to the beautiful deities of pagan mythology, took an active part."

[16] There seems to be disagreement about who actually wrote "The Maid of Monterrey." Lota M. Spell, in *Music in Texas* (Austin: Privately printed, 1936), pp 50–51, credits John H. Hewitt. J. Frank Dobie in "Ballads and Songs of the Frontier Folks," *Follow de Drinkin' Gou'd* (Folklore Society Publication No. VII, 1928), pp 160–162, credits James T. Lytle. The words in these two versions and the ones given here are almost identical.

The moonlight shone but dimly
Upon the battle plaine
A gentle breeze faned softly
Oer the features of the slain
The guns had hushed their thunder
The drums in silence lay
Then came the senorita
The Maid of Monterey.

She gave a look of anguish
On the dying and the dead
And she made her lap a pillow
For him who moaned and bled
Now heres to that bright beauty
Who drives deaths pangs away
That meek eyed senorita
The Maid of Monterey.

Although she loved her country
And prayed that it might live
Yet for the wounded foreigner
A tear she had to give
And when the dying soldier
In her bright gleam did pray
They blessed the senorita
The Maid of Monterey.

She gave the thirsty watter
And dressed each bleeding wound
A fervent prayr she uttered
For those whom death had doomed
And when the bugle sounded
Just at the break of day
They all blest the senorita
The Maid of Monterey.

CHAPTER X

Return from Mexico. Meeting Som of the Boys at San Antonio. Serving Out the Turm. Retireing to Private Life. Mooveing to Blanco. A Cold Snap. Receiveing Fire in a Mericalous Way. The Election. Takeing the Oath.

AFTER REMAINING in Monterey about two months I received dispatches for the department at San Antonio from Gen'l Tailor and set out for Texas, nothing occuring of any note on our homeward trip until ariveing at San Antonio. Sending my men into camp on the San Pedro Creek I hastened into town for provision, forage, etc. I arived oposite a grocery whare thare was ten or a dozen men loungeing round the door and I recognized Calvin Turner, Joe Williams, John Pickens, and John Sowell of McCullochs boys, and Bill Deadman, John Rogers, and Jim Roberts that was not of our company at the time.

I had not shaved for over four months and they did not recognize me until I spoke. I rode up and spoke and was in the act of alighting when the whole croud geathered me on their shoulders and started for a barbershop a block and a half away declareing it was shearing time.

I never touched the ground the whole way. They had me sheared, shaved, shampooned, and shirted. They geathered me again on their shoulders, carried me to an eating house, and ordered an oister supper. In the meantime they had my men suplied. These men had came with wagons for suplies for the company.

The next morning I turned my men over to the boys and set out for home and I remained with my family some two weeks and then set out to joine the command at San Marcos.

Soon after ariveing McCulloch was ordered to pitch his camp in Hamiltons Vally,[1] 60 miles above Austin, on the Colorado

---

[1] "Reminiscences of Jno. Duff Brown," in the *Quarterly of the Texas State Historical Association* (XII, No. 4 [April, 1909], p. 306), state: ". . . and in a few week

River. We served out the turm thare without seeing a track that a hostill Indian made and was mustered out th[e] 7th of October 1847 at Austin. Captain McCulloch raised another company and was stationed at the same place, but myself, Brother Soloman, John and Asa Sowell, Harden Turner, and Simon Cockrel and all the Seguin boys that had families left the servis.

After serving my country for near eleven years I thought I could retire with my family and let the young and single men do the rest of the soldering. On returning I bought land on the San Marcos River oposite the mouth of Plum Creek.² I worked at my trade most of the time, farming a little until 1859, about eleven years, in which time I had gotten up a good bunch of cattle, some 150 head, some 20 head of horses, and a good bunch of sheepe. After haveing two or three dry years togeather the range gave way so that I either had to sell off my stock or moove them to fresh range and I chose the latter and in the fall of 1859 I sold out my place, wound up my buisness, and set out to moove to Blanco County. That county had just been organized³ and the range was fresh. We got along all right until we struck the rough mountains between Millers Creek and Perdinalles river where it was up one side of a rough mountain and down the other side. We amerged into the vallies on the other side and went into camp.

Next morning the clouds seemed lowering and threatening rain and the weather was so unfavorable I sent the stock on with the two oldest boys and som hired help and my wife in the buggy with the three least children, thinking they could make it through to Frank Daniells by dark if no accident should happen. I knew that I could not make it, for I was driveing a long

---

¹ again entered the United States service as acting assistant surgeon for Captain H. E. McCulloch's Company. The Company was camped at Hamilton's Valley, fifty-five miles above Austin, in what was then Travis County, but is now Burnet. It was Captain McCulloch's second year at this station."

² See map of Gonzales County showing location of Nichols' land.

³ *The Handbook of Texas*, edited by Walter Prescott Webb and H. Bailey Carroll (2 vols., Austin: Texas State Historical Association, 1952), I, 172, tells of the origin of the county: "Blanco County was organized in 1858 from parts of Burnet, Comal, Gillespie and Hays Counties."

ox teem with a large wagon and a heavy loaded, but the stock
and buggy mad it all right but after dark.

I drove on, I had never traveled the road, but I could keep
the stock on the buggy tracks until about ten oclock it commenced a drizzleing rain. I had my son, Green, then a small boy
9 years old with me in the wagon. It soon rained so hard that
the sign of the stock and buggy was entirely obliterated and about
noon thare blewup a strong north wind and by two oclock the
ground and timber and everything was covered in sleete.

I had taken the rong road and crosed the branch whare Jonson
City now stands, went on until I struck the rough breakes of the
Perdenales River. I worked my way to the river at a place once
known as the Richard Cloute crossing and I found the river
greately swolen. It was then sundown and I camped and I was
so cold it was with great difficulty that I succeeded in belling,
hobbling, and turning my oxen out but I then began to look
around for som dry or dead wood to start a fire. I saw an old
postoak from which all the limbs had falen off and left a high
stump and the bark hung loose here and thare in long strips.
and I thought under this bark I might git som dry stuff to kindle
a fire with. I carried up all of the limbs but one, that one I thought
too heavy after lifting at the but end, though this was sota[4] dry
underneath the end, I broak som of the small limbs from it and
carried to the wagon.

I then went back to the old stump, pulled of som bark, and
underneath scratched of som rotten wood and taken a large piece
of bark and layed them down at the wagon and went for my
matches. I found them all wet, not one would ignite, and I then
went for my powder flint and steel which was in my shot pouch.
It was still raining and freezeing and I rumaged the wagon and
found my shot pouch upset and my powder horn stopper gone
my powder all run out in the wagon caused by the jolting o
the wagon over rough road.

Wat to do now I knew not. I paced the length of the wago

___
4 Nichols means "soda dry," or dry as soda—an old expression meaning very dry
soft and powdery like soda. It was a common pioneer expression.

back and forth. I thought of a way I had learned from the Indians of ketching fire by takeing two senia weeds,⁵ bore a hole
in the side of one, sharpen the end of the other and twirl it round
in my hands until it would git so hot it would take fire. I went
and hunted for som of these weeds but could not find any and
returned and commenced paceing again. It was now thick dark
and still raining and freezeing as fast as it fell and I went to the
wagon and asked my son if he was cold.

He says, "O, Pa! I am about to freeze to death."

At this time my top cloths was froze stiff on me and what could
I do for I was satisfide that I could not survive til morning with
my cloaths froze on me and the wagon sheete had leaked untill
all the bedding was froze stiff, and my son fast freezing to death
and all my own efferts and means exasted.

I commenced paceing again to try to keep from freezeing when
I fell into the following train of thoughts. Well, I once prayed
to the good God and he sent me watter and saved my life and the
lives of those that was withe me and he is the same God that he
was then, and the same that he was in Elijas day and perhaps
just as willing to help as he was then and at this juncture I fell
down on my marrowbones and asked God to manifest himself
to me in the power and strength of Elijas God and show forth
thy Great Power by Performing a merical in saveing the lives
of one whoes life thou hast spared and protected so long and in
so many close places, and that of my son who is young and tender and whoes life as yet is free from sin and now, o Lord God,
if it be consisteent with thy holy will and pleasure, now make
it manifest in som way that we may be saved from this dialemma
in to which we have fallen and let this cold wind scease and the
rain stop, the weather turn warm, or send us fire that we may
ive as thou didst send fire to consume the sacrafice that Elija

---

⁵ Robert A. Vines, in *Trees, Shrubs, and Woody Vines of the Southwest* (Austin:
University of Texas Press, 1960), pp. 545, 546, 547, describes Siene Weed as a type
of Sesbania, either Sesbania drummondii or Sesbania exaltata, both commonly called
Siene-weed or Rattlebox. It is a small shrub twelve to fifteen feet high, growing in
wet grounds and along streams, lakes, etc. Indians in Mexico made nets and fishlines
from fibers of the stems.

had prepared to be consumed by Thou sending fire from Heaven
to consume it to show the Prophets of Balle that Thou art God
and besides The thare are none else.

About here I thought of myself or could think of nothing els
to say and how long I was on my knees I do not know, but I do
know that it was with great difficulty that I rose to my feete, I
was so cold and stiff.

Once more on my feete I commenced paceing the length of
the wagon again but had not mad but one or two trips with my
head hung down when I heard a nois, a strange sound like fire
leaping six or eight feete from the ground and catching to a limb
of a tree full of dry leaves or like a large bird decending from a
great height with terrible velosity cutting the air with its wings.
The sound is hard to discribe, but maybe som of my readers has
heard som such sound. I looked in the direction of the old dead
stump as the sound proceded from that way and to my surprise I
saw a light blaze on the end of the old limb that I had lifted at
and thought too heavy to carry.

I gazed at it som time and my first thought was that I was
asle[ep] and dreaming but roused myself up and and found that
not the case and saw that it was a blaze in reality. I looked in-
tently to see if I could see anyone at the fire, and seeing no one
thare I knew then that it was sent in answer to my prayr.

I walked strait up to it and found the blaze flickering or flitting
around the but end of the limb with out consuming any of the
wood altho the wood was rotten or sota dry and soft on the under
side and was evidently not burning the wood as thare was no
smoke assending from the blaze, but I felt no heat from it altho
I felt warm and comfortable. I watched for two or three second
when I saw the blaze take hold of the wood and commence to
consume it, then the smoke began to assend and I was all right
then, I could feel the heat.

I knew I had backed out from carrying the limb at first, and
I thought it must go now. I went to the middle, picked it up as
though it would not weigh ten pounds, carried it to the wagon
and soon had a glowing fire. I went to the wagon, lifted my son

out and set him by the fire or rather laying him and by warming the wet bed clothes and raping him up in them hot, I soon succeeded in warming him and relieveing him and bringing him out of that stupor and sleep into which he had fallen and from which he never would have awoke without this timely aid. The rain now sceased and as we had eaten nothing sence early morn I went to cooking, and after supper we dryed our bedding, layed down, and slept until morning when we resumed our journey. I stoped seven miles above the town of Blanco on the river, rented a house, and was buisy the balance of the winter locateing my stock.

The next year thare was an election ordered to see whether or not the State of Texas would secede.[6] I had some redhot secesh neighbours who would frequently drop in to talk on this subject in order to find out my politicle views and I was frank in giveing my opinion in regard to the matter and would say we aught to wait and see what President Lincon and his cabinet is going to do. If they pass laws that is unconstitutional then they will be the aggressers and in that case then let us take up the Stares and Stripes and the Constatution and fight for our rights, and we will be successful. But on the other hand, if we secede, which I doubt our right to do under the Constitution, then we will be the aggresers, and they will have the right to coerce us back into the

6 Gammel, *Laws of Texas*, V, 347: "Extra Session of Eighth Legislature State of Texas, 1861. An Act to Provide for Submitting the Ordinance of Secession to a Vote of the People. *Section 1.* Be it enacted by the Legislature of the State of Texas, That the Chief Justices, or other county officers required by the directions of the State Convention, and presiding officers of precincts of the several counties of this State, are hereby empowered and required to order and to hold elections in their respective counties, and at their several precincts, on such day or days as may be provided therein, for the ratification or rejection of the Ordinance of Secession passed by a Convention of the people assembled in the City of Austin, on the 1st day of February, A.D. 1861, and conduct said elections in all respects according to the existing laws regulating elections for members of the Legislature, and make returns thereof in such manner and to such persons, and within such time, as may be prescribed by said Convention, under all the penalties prescribed in the laws aforesaid. *Section 2.* Be it further enacted, That all qualified electors for members of the Legislature of this State shall be entitled to vote at said election, at any precinct in the State, and indicate their approval or disapproval of said ordinance by the use of such terms as may be prescribed by said Convention. *Section 3.* That this Act take effect and be in force from and after its passage. Passed February 7, 1861."

A Foot-long Ballot

union which they will do for they have the Army, Navy and Treasury. Men and meanes is a great advantage to say nothing of the cause and if they dont want to put their own men in the field they can hire as many foureign soldiers as they want. They have all advantages of us.

One old man, my nearest neighbor, says, "Then you will vote to stay in the Union and sit on the stool of do nothing and let them run over us and take our rights away from us."

I never went to town but what I was tackled by someone and I spent my opinion freely, thinking every man had a right to do so, always advocating the union principles and was pounced on by some one as though I was the only Union man in the county. Thare was plenty others, but they kept their mouths shut as I should have done. I must acknowledg tho that I was a little contrary, for in 1845 I voted against anexation, believeing it best for Texas to remain a seperate, independent Republic, but after anexation I found it worked well enough and I become satisfide and could see no good that would accrew from seceding. If it was an eror in me it was an eror of the head and not of the heart.

The day of election was but a few days off, and I went to town on som buisness and thare was a large croud assembled at the grocery whare thare was big talking and biger drinking.

I stood round awhile haveing nothing to say when one fellow sideled up close to me in order that I might hear him and said, "Well, boys, the election is close by, and thare is a big croud of us has agreed to meete on the ground early and Ill venture a treat for this croud that a union man wont venture to show his head at the poles on that day. We have agreede that if any dare come we will clean um up as fast as they come, and well do it hore."

The croud hurrahed for Ike. I said nothing but thought thare would be one union vote cast if but one. When the day came I went down early and taken a slip of paper about a foot long and wrote it full from one end to the other, "for the Union" and when the poles was opened I handed it in without folding it up. They taken it, looked at it, showed it to all the judges and clerks, then folded it up, and deposited it in the box, regestered my name, and put on my ticket, "Nomber 1," and I went out.

They had hoisted the bonny blue flag that beares a single star and I stood round catching items but said nothing. Presently I saw a large croud comeing in, and when they came near they commenced fireing at the flag and it came near causing a serious difficulty, but we got it settled after a while and the result was, thare was a large majority of votes cast for the union at that box that day,[7] but when the final result was known and the state had seceded I saw that I had the sow by the wrong ear but then I should have sided in and been content had they let me alone and not bullyraged and teased me and called me a black republican. One man, a large stock owner, said to my face that a Union man should not live in the county in peace.

I says, "How are you going to help yourself. What you going to do."

He said nothing but he showed me in the end. After the election the Confederal was organized and in the year 1861 the war commenced. Thare was a man appointed in every county to administer the oath of allegiance to the Confederate government and Co'l Duff[8] was apointed for this purpose in Blanco County and he apointed a day and the majority met and taken the oath.

He left another apointment but I still did not attend. I had a blacksmith shop and wood shop and I worked away and bothered no boddy. About the fourth trip that he mad, as he comanded a

[7] Election returns for February 23, 1861, showed "*Blanco County, For Secession* 86, *Against* Secession 170" (William Winkler, *Journal of the Secession Convention of Texas, 1861* [Austin: Texas Library and Historical Commission, 1912], p. 88).

[8] James M. Duff was a Scottish adventurer and soldier of fortune who had been in the United States Army at one time and had been drummed out because of his actions. He professed to be an ardent Confederate and soon was a colonel in command of a unit of Texas Partisan Rangers. He was ordered by Governor Francis Lubbock and General H. P. Bee to administer the oath of allegiance to the Confederacy in Blanco, Gillespie, Kerr, Medina, and Kendall counties. Duff left Texas after the Civil War and later died in Paris, France. See Guido E. Ransleben, *A Hundred Years o Comfort in Texas* (San Antonio: Naylor Co., 1954), p. 121; Claude Elliott, "Union Sentiment in Texas," *Southwestern Historical Quarterly*, L, No. 4 (April, 1947) 463–464.

company on the fronteer, he got every man but myself and one other man, and he apointed another day. All this time I was waited on, worned and threatened, but I told them that I never would take the oath until I was forsed to do so, and it went on this way for some months.

About this time the head leaders of the secesh party formed a ring or town click with this big stock owner for President in order to have things go their own way. They had regular mass meeting as they called them,[9] but I never attended one of them and soon after one of these meeting[s] I was notefide that Co'l Duff would be thare on a certain day, and that I had better be thare and take the oath.

I paid no atention to the time, so the next day after the day apointed, I was buisy at work in the shop and saw the Co'l and two other men drive up and git out of the hack loaded down with arms and I thought to myself, "Gone up now." They came to the shop and told their business, and I says, "Well, gentlemen, I have said I would not take the oath without I was forsed to and I concidder a forse-put no-put atal so out with your oath." Duff administered the oath and all left.

[9] There were considerable differences in the feelings of Texans concerning participation in the Civil War. In all probability only about one third of the people were staunch Confederates, and a large number did not want to secede at all. Of those several areas in Texas that were predominantly loyal to the Union, one of the strongest included Blanco, Gillespie, Kendall, Kerr, and Llano counties. After war actually started, many went into Confederate service, because of their allegiance to their state or their families, or because their feelings were not strong and it was easier to join than to stay out. Some, like Nichols, did not want to secede and took the Confederate oath only when forced to do so. Those who were steadfast Unionists went into hiding or, if they could, left the state. Few people in Texas really expected or desired to go to war over secession.

CHAPTER XI

Raids by Indians in Blanco County. Stealing Horses. Wounding a Negro Boy. Chaceing Mrs. Daniell and a Negro Woman. Killing Three Children and Wounding Mrs. Youngblood. Killing a Negro Man. Chaceing Two Men. Chaceing One Man. One Indian Kiled. Killing Sheppeard, His Wife, and Child Boy Missing. Death of Tom Felps and Wife. Death of Dollahide and Son. Scalp Dance. Day and Nickelsons Fight with Indians. Wounding a Young Lady. Two Boys Chased. Two Men Wounded. Death of Two Women and Five Children. Scalping a Woman Alive. Capture and Death of Two Girls. Death of Rowland Nichols.

In the spring of this year 1862 the Indians became very troublesome in Blanco County owing, it was supposed, to so many men being absent in the war. They mad a raid early this spring about 30 in number comeing down, ran on to Dick Hudsons negro boy who was herding sheepe for Dr. Asig,[1] wounding him several times. The boy ran and the Indians after him and they chased him several hundred yards when the boy took refuge in a pen built around a spring and lay flat down in the mud and water. The redskins came up and seeing him laying in thare, thrust their lances in him several times inflicting several ugly wounds and left him for dead.

They went on, crossed the river, and on up to Hudsons house there being no one at the house but Frank Daniells wife with two children and Hudsons negro women with two small children. no [other] person on the place. As Daniell had to go to Gonzales County on buisness, he had taken his family to Hudsons to stay during his absence, Hudson and his brother-in-law, Robert Davis

---

[1] Dr. Assig is listed by John Striblin Moursand in *Blanco County Families for 100 Years* (Austin: Privately printed, 1958), p. 11: "Dr. Adolph Assig was to become a resident of Blanco County in later years, the late 1860's and early 1870's."

being on a cowhunt, and Mrs. Hudson had gone soon that morning to a neighbours to worke a piece of cloth, the two women, seeing the Indians first, geathered their children, ran into the house, and bared the doors and crawled under the bed. The redskins rode up to the house as thare was no yard fence to prevent them, and peeped in at the cracks on all sides but could see no one, suposed thare was no one at home, rode round several times but soon espied a bunch of Hudsons saddle horses hobbled out a short distance from the house and mad for them.

Takeing the advantage of this temporary absence of the savages, the women taken their children and left the house and started for Walter Smiths house whare Mrs. Hudson had gone. They had to cross the river and in order to do so afoot they had to go som distance below to som falls. The Indians discovered them makeing their escape and gave chace, ran them a close race, but the women made it to the falls first and the Indians, after sending a shower of arrows after them but to no effect, they turned back as they could not cross at that place horseback.

The women went on and met Mrs. Hudson and told their story and Mrs. Hudson turned back and they all went to Smiths and late in the evening Dr. Asag called at Smiths on a professional visit and was informed of the facts. He said he had a large stone house and for feare of another attact, they had better all git togeather at his house at least for the night, so they all repaired thither. As Dr. Asag and the croud went on to his house they had to pass the mud spring whare Bunk, the wounded negro, was and as they passed Bunk hailed them and Asag took him in his buggy, toaken him on, dressed his wounds, etc.

About dark Hudson came home, found the doors open and fire burning and suposed his folks was on a visit [and] would be home soon, and being hungry, cooked and eate his supp[er] and waited awhile longer. He began to feel uneasy and sucspe[ct]ing something had went wrong and knowing that one of Smiths ch[i]ldren was sick, he suposed they must be thare and never one thought entered his head that Indians was the cause, saddled his horse aga[i]n, mounted and rode over to Smiths and in his anksiety to learn the truth left everything at home as he had found them.

On ariveing at Smiths he found the doors shet and bared, and
more puzzeled than ever, he turned and rode to Asags and thare
he learned the story.

Rock Creek emtied into the Perdenales River a few hundred
yards below Hudsons house[2] and Frank Daniell lived three or
four miles above on this creek. He had been to Gonzales County
for a load of corn and had left his wagon with the driver and
early that morning set out for home. After rideing hard, arived
at his ranch about dark and after makeing som arangements at
the ranch, he set out for Hudsons whare his family had been
staying during his absents. On his way down he passed near a
camp fire and heard loud laughing and talking but payed no
more attention to it suposeing it to be a lot of cowboys camped
thare.

He arived at Hudsons a few minutes after Hudson left and
found the doors open and fire burning. Frank tried to take in the
situation but every surmise seemed to fail to answer his purpose.
Finely he fixed it up that someone in the neighborhood must
bee dangerously ill and that someone would be back soon, and
being in the same fix that Hudson was, hungry, he serched the
place over for something to eat but found nothing but a small
piece of bread still warm, so he taken that and a cup of milk and
parcially satisfide his hunger.

After remaining an hour and no one put in an apearance, he
too began to feel uneasy. He mounted again his tired horse, and
as it was very dark and the ford to Asags, the nearest house, dread-
ful bad to cross even in day time, he concluded to go up the river
two or three miles opisit the second house and cross as that was a
better ford. After wandering around for some time he found the
ford and crossed over to the house of Mr. Freemans.

He hollowed several times before he could arouse any of the
inmates but finely Mrs. Freeman came to the door and he told
her his story. She said she knew of no one sick in the neighbour-
hood, she knew of no Indians in, but neither of them could solve

---

[2] Hudson's home is placed in the same general location by Moursand (*ibid.*, p
200): "It is believed that this land grant and the place of residence of R. B. Hudson
was in the Rocky vicinity of Blanco County, Texas, near the Perdernales River."

the problem. She said Mr. Freeman, Hudson, and Davis was all out on a cowhunt, and it was late, and he had better stop and stay til morning and Frank excepted her invitation and stayed til morning.

Next morning as soon as he could see his way, he was once more in the saddle, and on his way to try to solve the mistery and soon met Dick Hudson who unfolded to him the whole matter. He had started to see if Freemans family was safe and learning that all was well in that respect, he turned back with Frank. They raised a few men and trailed the redskins up Rocky Creek to whare they had camped, a thing I never knew of a band of Indians doing before, it was their camp that Frank had passed the night before and suposed it cowhunters. They followed their trail, found whare they had rounded up a large bunch of horses, kiled one, and left the settlements. Mrs. Freeman never heard of the disturbance for a week after it hapened.

At another time about a month later the Indians mad another raid when Brother John Nichols and his s[on] Andrew was up from Guadaloupe Co. at my house on som buisness. After supper we ware sitting out doores talking when we heard the sound of horses feete runing and at the same time smeled the Indian cent. Any boddy that is acostom to the cent can decide readyly. We ran out into the prairie whare their horses was last seen but too late, the Indians had already taken both his horses and one of mine and about 18 head of horses that I had in charge for another man. Next morning we trailed them until they struck the rough mountain devide, but we had to abandon persuit as they could out travel us in rough country.

In the following spring 1863 the Indians mad another raid down the country near New Braunfels, stole som horses, and kiled a German boy that was out herding sheepe, turned back, came up on Little Blanco or Southfork, rounded up about 70 head of good horses belonging to William Jonas, passed near the town of Blanco and on accross the Perdinalles River near Hudsons, and out up Willow Creek until they arived at the house of Mrs. Youngblood. Two of her children, a girl 12 and a boy 10 years old, was at the spring geathering watercress sallad when

Indians came upon them and attempted to capture the girl. She, having a butcherknife which she used in cutting the salad, with this weapon she fought them so corageously that they had to kill her. By the time the boy had nearly reached the house shouting at the top of his voys for his maw to run to his assistance, and the widow hearing her sons shouts ran out of the house just in time to see the savages kill him.

She ran back into the house, shut and bared the door and prepared to defend herself, having one rifle, one double barrel shot gun, and two six shooters, all well and fresh loaded in the house. The savages then attact the house. They all dismounted and serounded the house about 30 in nomber and leaveing a [guard] with their horses, they tried the door, but it was secure[ly] fastened. One of the redskins, seeing a hole near the door, which had been left to thrust the hand in to unbolt the door, h[e] ventured to peepe in when the woman, seeing his hidiou[s] face through the hole, she had been holding her rifle directly to that place, she fired. Her shot taken efect near the left eye and he fell like a quarter of beef. From the top [of] the house another came forward but on seeing her with [a] gun pointed thare he withdrew his gaze.

The redskins th[en] made a desperate efort to brake down the door but failed. One of them went round to the chimney corner and p[un]ched out a chinkin and then they had two holes to peepe in at so when they would look in at one place and she would point her gun at him he would dodge back and the other one would shoot his arrows in at her and by that means they succeeded in wounding her severarly, the arrow entering on one side of her left breast and following round to the shoulder blade the spike comeing out through the skin. Nothing discouriaged by this, having her gun ready the next time one darkened the hold she spoiled his painted face by filling it full of buckshot and he fell back kerplumix. The other one, thinking she would have to reload, peeped in and she served him the same way with the other load.

She now had recorse to her sixshooters which caused some delay and in this delay they flocked to the portholes and shot near a hundred arrows into the house at her, killing her infant who was on the bed asleepe. Being weake from loss of blood and not being an expert with the six shooter as she was with the guns, it gave them a better chance to shoot their arrows. After emtying her rifle, shot gun, and five barrels of one six shooter and the savages, failing in every attempt to enter the house, drew off carrying off their dead and wounded with them.

Sam Debusk, a young man that was staying with the widow and who had been out stockhunting at the time, returned after the Indians had been gone about ten minutes, and after extracting the arrows from the woman and dressing her wounds and giveing the boy and girl a passing glance, set out to their nearest neighbour som two miles for help which lay in the direction the Indians had gone.[3] He rode rapidly expecting to find his neighbors massecreed or find the Indians in the act. He had not proceded fare on his way before he came upon the mangled boddy of a negro man he had hired makeing rails, and procedeing rapidly on his journey found his neighbours unmolested.

[3] Sowell (*Early Settlers and Indian Fighters*, pp. 737–738) gives a slightly different version of this incident: "In 1864 Mr. Fessenden moved to Blanco County and settled on Hickory Creek. Three miles from him on Grape Creek lived the family of Youngblood. He had died and a man named Sam DeBuss was a hired hand on the place, but at the time of which we write he was away. Three of the children, a boy and two girls—were about a quarter of a mile from the house when the Indians came upon them. They soon killed the boy, and the girls ran swiftly towards the house, followed by the Indians, who kept shooting at them with arrows until both were wounded, but they succeeded in getting into the house, the mother holding the door open for them and screaming for them to 'Run! run! run!' during the desperate race. There were two rifles in the house, and Mrs. Youngblood took up one of these and at once commenced a battle with the Indians. They succeeded in getting to the door and were trying to force it open when the brave woman killed one of them. After firing both guns the woman would pick up first one and then the other, and present it when they advanced and the Indians would skip back around the corner. There were six of them when they came to the house and when they left and were last seen only five were together, but what they did with the one who fell in the yard and they carried away could not be ascertained. Up to the time the Indians left the mother had no time to attend to her wounded children, but now pulled the arrows out of them. One was shot in the head and the other in the body. Both got well, but the one wounded in the head was ever after partially deranged. DeBuss came back before night and went out and brought the body of the little boy in. He was 10 years of age, and the girls were 8 and 6. After night DeBuss came to the house of Mr. Fessenden and waked him up and told him the news and they went to the camp of the rangers on Cypress Creek and aroused them."

After burrying the dead children and negro man, a croud was raised to follow the savages, but too late as the savages had too much the start. But on their trail it was found that they had burried five of their nomber in one grave or gully.

In the fall of this same year I taken my wagon and team, two of my boys, and John Richbourg, a cousen to my wife by marriage, and went out up the river 8 or 10 miles prep[ar]ed to camp out in order to kill and bring in a large wild beef which I had runing up thare and which could not be drove, and Richbourgs wife came over to my house in order to have company, that night turned her horse in the field whare my wifes mare and colt was.

We found, kilt and dressed our beef and awhile after dark we heard a croud of men passing down on the opisit side of the river from our camp laughing and talking. Suposing it to be a croud of cowhunters returning emty handed, we thought no more about it for awhile until they traveled round a bend of the river and we got the wind of them, then knew it was Indians by the scent. They went on down and taken the horses out of the field letting the fence down in thirty stepes of the house. The women saw heard and smelt them but could do nothing.

The redskins went on down the river, som on one side, som on the other, geathering horses, and when they had rounded up near a hundred head they turned and taken the rough devide and departed hence in peace.

About ten days after this my son Dan had been out on a horse hunt, returning about dark, put up his horse, a big fine stalion that I had, fed him, and when done eating his corn went to stake him out to grass. He tied him to a bush and started back to house. After gitting forty or fifty yeards he heard horses runing but suposed it was som lose horses coming in to water, went on. Next morning he went out to git the hors but the Indians go him first. The horse had not bit a mouthful of grass until he had been taken.

They rode that horse five miles below Dripping Springs to James Robertses ranch a distance of thirty five miles and geathered horses as they went and they must have rode the horse 50 or 60 miles that night. This James Roberts was a son of Buck

Roberts mentioned els whare as being one of the first settlers of Seguin, and Jim had a horse ranch with several hundred head of horses on it and was geathering his horses for the purpose of branding his colts and also intending to take off a drove of ponies to sell. He was hurding out in daytime and pening at night and how the Indians came to know this is a mistrey to me unless thare was some reinagade white man or Mexi[can] with them, as they never halted from the time they left my place until they arived at Roberts Ranch about an hour befor day. They opened the gate and turned out the whole drove, som 250 head, taken them northwards toward Shingle Hill and mad the landing safe without a wave of trouble roll accross their peaceful breasts. They left my horse on their trail, given out and so kild up that he was never of any servis to me afterwards.

In the spring of 1865 the war had closed and the soldiers began to return and amongst the rest Frank Daniell. After remaining at home some weeks Frank and Richbourg started out on a horse hunt. They rode upon the side of a mountain to spy out for the horses, and after looking round in every way in the distance in vain they discovered the horses but a short distance from them in a small glade almost serounded by a dens thickete of underbrush, and thinking the horses had taken shelter in thare from the flys which was very bad, they turned and rode directly toward them.

The horses being directly between them and home, they rode lasurely along and appreached within 80 to 100 yards when all at once 15 or 20 Indians charged out of the brush and dashed up towards them yelling like demons. Seeing themselves cut off from home they wheeled their horses at right angles and mad for a deepe wide ravine near a mile distant, closely persued by the redskins.

Richbourg had no fire arms and Frank had the army six shootor and told Richbourg to take the leade and pick his way and he would follow and watch the Indians, and when the Indians would charge up to close, Frank would raise his pistol and point towards them and they would hold up.

Once when the savages were crouding them close in a rough

piece of ground, Richbourg was in the act of losing his hat by its being blown off his head but succeeded in catching it in his hand and did not replace it on his head, displaying the large prairie on his head, haveing only 75 or 80 hairs on his head and them low down on the back of his neck. The hot sun shineing on the scalp mad his head glisten and left the sad impression in the savage breast that he had already been scalped. All at once they stoped short and broak out into a harty loud laugh and turned back, still laughing and jabering. It is now reduced to a certainty that John, haveing no scalp, saved both of their lives for they suposed Frank was in the same fix and the savages went back, taken all of the horses, and was happy, and Frank and John breathed easy.

Later on in this same year Preston Shepeard, his wife and child and her brother Thomas Huckaboy, then a lad 12 or 13 years old, was all returning from Lockhart horseback. After crossing Little Blanco or Southfork, assended a ridge and was attacted by Indians, who kilt and scalped Shepeard, his wife and child, and it seems that while this horrowble deed was being inacted, Tom Huckeboy, being mounted on a good pony, ran off but was soon overtaken, that is from all indications as his hat and half of his coat was found on the trail and several miles farther on the trail part of his shirt and pieces of his other clothing was found, but the fate of the boy was never known as he was never found or heard of afterwards.[4]

In the spring of 1866 the Indians mad a raid down through Blanco County. My son George, Clem Hinds, Tom Felps, and others ware out on the divide trying to pen some wild horses, some 30 or 40 head that had not been in a pen for five years and this croud of men, 12 or 15, had built a pen and was trying to run them into it. Part of the men was left at the pen, part went in search of the horses to start them, and George and Hinds was

---

[4] "Letter from J. W. Speer to E. M. Pease" and "Statement of Indian Depredations in Blanco County," both in *Texas Indian Papers, 1860–1916* (4 vols., Texas State Archives), IV, 265, 326, give accounts of the killing of the Shepherds and Tom Huckabee by the Indians.

stationed out on the high divide waiteing for others to run the horses by, when they would put in on fresh horses and pen them.

Of corse they had their eyes skined and on the lookout in every direction not knowing which way the horses would come when George saw a bunch of men comeing directly towards them and says, "Yonder they come," pointing to the bunch of men.

Hinds being more experienced, after looking a few seconds says, "George, that is not the boys, that is Indians."

They mounted their horses and started for the pen whare five or six of the boys ware waiting to help pen the horses. They all mounted and set out in a gallope but the redskins had left the divide and taken to the river vally and across the county towards Currys Creek.

Their course lay down the Naturel Bridge Creek and near the natural bridg they ran on to Sam Gray Sr. and chaced him up a good lot, makeing him feel for his scalp several times in the chace to see if he had lost it. They continued their way up Crab Apple Creek and over the divide to the head of Currys Creek and halted in a dence thicket until nightfall, then emerged from their hideing place and continued their course to Westly Callahans, a son of Captain Callahans, and taken a fine buggy horse from Westly. The horse was tied to the galrey post and a large bull dog lying on the galrey. Westly said he never could account for the way them Indians taken that horse from thare without that dog finding them out but such was the case.

Then they went on over to Dr. Nowlens, but it being the right stage of the moon, they was prepared for them at that place. The Dr. had his horses in the pen and a man and a boy 12 or 13 years old, an orfen that Dr. Nowlen was raiseing, lying in the crib with the door open, and both were armed with good double barrel shot guns, well loaded and instructed not to hail. The Indians let the lot fence down at the back side and one came in to drive the horses out and came near the crib door when the boy, without saying a word to the other man, raised his gun and fired, the shot takeing effect in his back, killing him instantly. The other redskins turned and fled leaveing their dead comrad at the mercy of the palefaces but froze to Callahans horse.[5]

On another occaision in this same year, Dave Wanslow was cutting ceder som distance from whare he was liveing and rode to his work. One morning he staked his horse at the edg of the brak and resumed his labors as usuel, and about ten oclock he heard the sound of horses feete near whare his horse was tied. He ran to the edg of the breake to see what was the mater and was just in time to see 15 or 20 Indians take his horse and for them to see him and give chace but Dave knew the country and taken the rough ceder round whare the redskins could not ride. In that way he made his escape. As Dutch John used to say, "Mit a tam tied squeeze." He went in to the settlement on Millers and Yagers Creeks and raised a squad of men, 8 or 10 in nomber, and followed on their trail which was very plain as the redskins had collected up a good bunch of horses.

The citizens followed them on to the head of Rocky Creek and came in sight of them and the Indians stoped and beconed to them to come on. The citizens went on within one or two hundred yards of the Indians, saw the redskins were not going to run

[5] Sowell (*Early Settlers and Indian Fighters*, pp. 699–700) gives a different and more detailed account of this same incident: "At the time Dr. Nowlin had two young men hired, named Francis Keiser and Charley Williams, and put them on guard at his horselot at night. He had gathered up his best horse stock and put some of them in a small pasture near by and locked others in stables. In the early part of the night it was evident Indians were around on account of the commotion among the horses in the pasture. The Indians were in there after them, and had made gaps in the fence and were trying to drive them out, but the horses would not run by these places. The two boys on guard at the lot got in a corncrib with their guns and thought best to remain quiet and await developments, but as the night wore on they fell asleep. About two o'clock in the morning the Indians failing to get the horses out of the pasture, two of them came to the lot to see what chance there was of getting some there. They took down the fence to the field lot and orchard, so they could get out easy if discovered. About this time a dog on the place discovered the presence of the Indians and set up a furious barking which awakened little Kate Nowlin and she began to cry. At this time the two young men were fast asleep at their post in the crib. The Doctor waked up and told his little daughter not to cry as the dogs would not hurt her and to go to sleep again. But all at once the stillness of the night was broken by "Bang, Bang," in the direction of the corncrib. Dr. Nowlin sprang clear into the middle of the floor and seizing his gun ran out. . . . The barking of the dog had awakened the boys, and looking out through a crack they saw the two Indians by moonlight. . . . The ball from Keiser's gun struck the Indian at whom he aimed in the top of the head and he fell, but Williams was a little slower to fire and his Indian started to run and he missed him. He made his escape."

and halted, thinking the Indians would probably charge them
but the savages then only dared them by beconing them to come
on. The citizens went no farther but held a consultation and concluded that the Indians was too strong for them and the redskins,
seeing the citizens was not going to attact them, turned themselves round, bent low on their horses and pated themselves at
the boys and slowly mooved on.

The boys turned back, som to Blanco, som to the settlements
on Rocky, and collected a croud of about 30 men includeing myself, my son George and Frank Daniell. We followed on their
trail two days, but they kept the rough devide between the Guadalupe and Perdeanalles and out traveled us and we had to abandon pursuit.

Again in the spring of 1867 a band of Indians mad a raid
down the country and returning through Blanco County mad
their way accross the Perdinalles River and up the Cypres Fork.
Tom Felps by this time had married and was living on that
stream and having a wild horse staked out, told his wife he was
going to moove his horse and then try his luck fishing and started
off. His wife, after quieting her child to sleepe, left it in care of
its grandmother, taken her fishing tackle and set out to join her
husband in a social fishing frolic. It was not known how long
they remained fishing but from the string of fish which lay near
they must have enjoyed their sport for an hour or two when the
Indians came upon them, kiled and scalped Felps and near a
hundred yards they had overtaken, kiled and scalped Mrs. Felps[6]
and went on a mile or two, chaced and overtaken a boy 12 or 13
years old, lifted him from his horse, set him on his feete on
the ground unharmed, taken the horse and persued their journey. Som six or eight miles further on they ran on to old man
Dollahide and his son going from Round Mountain whare the

6 Wilbarger (*Indian Depredations in Texas*, p. 643) says this murder occurred in
1868.
  Moursand (*Blanco County Families for 100 Years*, p. 120) says: "Thomas C.
Felps, born in Tennessee on November 10, 1834, married Eliza V. White, daughter
of S. T. White. He and his wife were killed by the Indians on July 21, 1869, at the
S. T. White place on Cypress Creek east of Round Mountain, Texas."
  "Statement of Indian Depredations in Blanco County," *Texas Indian Papers*,
1860–1916 (IV, 326), gives the date as July 22, 1869.

old man had been teaching scool, chaced them, overtaken, kild and scalped them both[7] and traveled on in the path of peace with none to molest or make them afraid.

Thare was a party followed them next day but never overtaken them, but found whare they had camped all night, and as they had four scalps they had a scalp dance. Now, my readers, as I have mentioned these dances several times in my book and scalp dances is nombered with the things of the past, but few men now liveing ever saw one, and as I have seen many caried on by the Tonkaway and Lipan tribes and two by the Comanchie tribe and suposing that all tribes carry on their scalp dances alike, I will indeaver to discribe the way they are carried on.

When a band of Indians is succesful in obtaining scalps they stop and camp, streatch a rope round in a circle, drive a stake in the center, then tie the scalps to an arrow without a spike and the oldest warior takes the stick of scalps and enters the ring, the rest standing on the outside.

They then all commence singing, "Ha yah noh ha noh non nah nah na nah," and repeat this all the time. One is inside, he stands about one third bent forward and jumps both feete at a time off the ground, and strains every nerve to keepe from mooveing his boddy and the one that ca[n] jump both feete off the ground and hit himself with his heels the oftenest without mooveing his boddy is the best dancer and is intitled to wear the scalps to his belt for so many days and they keep on at this until all the wariors have waved the stick of scalps and danced his turn. When there is women with them they too sing but not dance.

Later on in this same year Henry M. Day, a son of Milford Days, his wife, and two children, her father, Brackston Nickelson, and a single daughter, Lucinda Nickelson, was all returning home from Fredricksbourg whare they had been tradeing

[7] These murders are also recounted in other sources:

"January 1870. Dollohite & son (names and ages not ascertained) were shot with Balls and some arrows found on the spot, this took place on Cypress" (*ibid.*, p. 327)

"Wesley Dollahite, and uncle of W. W. Dollahite, was a teacher at Roun Mountain and he and his son were killed by Indians in 1870" (Moursand, *Blanc County Families for 100 Years*, p. 448).

all in a two horse wagon when in a few miles of home was attacted by 25 or 30 Indians. The redskins charged the wagon and
sent a shower of arrows seemingly suficient to have kild twice
their nomber and strange to say no one was hurt. Day and Nickle-
son was both armed with Winchester rifles, but their position
being so exposed in the wagon they concluded to take shelter
behind some trees that stood near by.

Mrs. Day, having one child in her arms, she leaped from the
wagon leaveing the other one sitting on the seat suposing her
husband would take care of him. But the husband, in his ank-
ziety for the safety of his family, grabed his gun and went to
shooting and did not notice the child and Mrs. Day taken the
nerest tree she could see. They all left the wagon and taken to
the trees, the Indians sending shower after shower of arrows
after them. By this time the two men had got their fire arms in
order and was using them to good effect.

The old man, seeing one Indian runing straight from him,
says, "Blast him. Now look mit whare his galeses would cross,"
and fired, and the redskin was seen to clutch his horses neck and
ran but a short distance and fell. They then mad a charge with
their whole force in order to try and dislodge the whites and capture the wagon. The two men fired so rapidly they succeeded in
repelling the charge but the savages had som rifles and used
them very dextariously. The tree that the young lady had se-
lected was a large roughbarked blackjack and the Indians in
shooting at her put a dozen balls in the tree and one glanceing
shot struck near the right breast, wounding her conciderabely.

The Indians now made another desperate charge to capture
the wagon and horses but was falling thick and fast by the un-
earing aim of the two men but would rally and charge again.
Mrs. Day, watching the contest going on around the wagon, discovered her little boy still sitting on the wagon seat whare she
had left him, very composely and unhurt serounded by savage
foes. She screamed and ran to him and just as the wagon began
to moove off with a savage on each side of the horses to whip
them up, she snatched her child from its perilous situation, and

"She snatched her child from its perilous situation"

mad good her retreat back to her tree and other child amid loud yells and a shower of arrows and bullets. If the father or the grandfather had ever discovered the child in its perilous situation it was not mad known but knowing that it would indanger their own lives as well as that of the woman and other child to venture thare, but the woman hisitated not a moment to imperil her own life for that of her child.[8]

The savages ran the horses and wagon off a few hundred yards and straddled a tree, dismounted, cut the harness off the horses, takeing such of the straps, lines, etc., as they thought they could use in their buisness, and helped themselves to such of the goods in the wagon as suited [them and] taken both horses. While all this was going on the two men had exausted the amunition in their magazenes and had to replnish, giveing the savages an oppertunity to remoove their dead and wounded off the field which they did in a hurry and left the citizens masters of the situation, a little the worse in mind and purse but all able to hoof it home, now and then feeling the top of their heads to assertain if their scalps was still thare.

On another occaision Henry Aten and George Haselette, two boys, ware out stockhunting and the Indians, 10 or 15 in nomber, discovered them and gave chace. The boys broke to run, the redskins in hot pursuit and for the firs two miles it was doubtful whether the boys would make their escape and save their scalps or be over taken and loose them. The thought of looseing their scalps mad them exert every nerve in both man and horse, and for the first mile it was lickitabrindle who would and who should, but the boys kept about the same distance between them, but the next mile the ground was rough and uneaven and the savages began to gain on them and with loud yells of exultation was gaining on them at every jump and it was now nip and tuck. The boys knew the country ahead of them and mad a circurious run around the head of a steepe ravine and the redskins seeing them

[8] This account of Indian attack on the Henry Day family has been verified by Mrs. Evelyn Porter Kaufman of Phoenix, Arizona, a granddaughter of Henry and Priscilla Nicholson Day. Mrs. Kaufman says the story has been told to each generation of the family.

make a turn, they endeavered to gain on them by cutting through but struck the deep rough ravine whare they could not cross and abandoned pursuit.

On the run Henry lost his hat and when they found the Indians had gave up the chace they slacked their gait and rode up close togeather and George says, "Henry, whare is your hat."

Henry says, "I lost it in the run. Do you supose a man could be chaced two miles by the Indians through the brush and the Indians steping on his heels every jump and not loose his hat."

George says, "No. By golly!" and pulled his hat off and threw it as fare as he could send it, and said, "The Indians run me a close race too," and soon after the boys slacked up in a trot and breathed easy.

Again still later on in this same year the Indians mad another raid down the country about thirty or forty in nomber but was discovered going down. Thare was 12 or 15 of the settlers go togeather including George and Dan Roberts, both sons of Buck Roberts, and set out in persuit and near whare Jonson City now stands overtaken and ingagued them in battle. The Indians discovered the settlers and took position, and the boys charged them in their position. The firs[t] charge George Roberts received a wound accross his nose cuting the skin on each cheek but kept on his gallant fighting. The boys mad five or six successfull charges with the enevetable Winchester rifles and at every charg could be seen several redskins to bite the ground but haveing about half their nomber armed with rifles and the rest good bowmen and outnombering the whites two or three to one, they was hard to dislodge but on every charge the boys could see some Indian or horse fall.

The boys concluded to make one desperate effort to dislodge the savages chargeing into their lines and fighting them in close quarters for some minuts, fell back and in this charge Dan Roberts received a sevear wound in the thigh, the same shot wou[n]d[ing] his horse fataly so that after retiring to a small [clump of] liveoak brush and while examining and dressing hi wound, [the Indians] taken the advantage of this pause in th [fight to remoove] their dead and wounded suposed to be hal [dead, and] left for parts unknown and whites did not follow.

In the fall of the same year [the Indians] returned [to the] Northern potion of Blanco County. In the settlement known as Mission Valley lived Mr. Butler, Mr. Dancer, Mr. Friend, Mr. Forester, the two Jonson brothers, and others. The men nearly all being out on a hog hunt, Mrs. Friend, Mrs. Forister, and her daughter went to the house of one of the Mr. Jonsons for the purpose of spining some stocking yarn and about 3 oclock in the evening two Indians entered the house one at each door and says, "Me want squaw," and grabed a young lady, Miss Forester, the other a girl of 12 years old. The cry was raised and the three women armed themselves, one with a smoothing iron, the other two with chairs, let in on the savages and felled them both and would have dispatched the two savages but for the interfearance of about a dozen other savages entering the house and rescued their comrades by shooting the three women, killing two of them dead.

Then after killing five children of diffrent ages, proceded to scalp the three women, taken the scalps of the other two and when they came to Mrs. Friend, they geathered up her long hair, cut round the edge of the hair all round, then placed one foot on her neck and gave a jerk, tearing all the skin and hair from her head. She was not dead but fained death, and said she neither mooved, groaned or schringed but lay as still as death.

After comiting this bloody deede they tied the young lady and the girl, left the house, captured a boy 9 or 10 years old, and started on through the valley. After traveling a few miles they kild and scalped the boy. Crossing over the top of a ceder mountain they left the young lady dead and scalped, and she had been cruely outraged and her mangled body lay on the ground with her feete and hands tied to stakes. It was suposed that she faught them so they had to kill her. So[mewhat] farther on the trail they left the girl in the same fix. [When] the savages had been gone som hours Mrs. Friend crawled, as she could not walk, being wounded in the thigh, out of the house and looking in every direction to be convinced that the savages was gone and being very ankcious to know the fate of her little ones at home concluded to try and crawl home, a mile and a half distant. With a brisk north wind blowing and the ground half covered in snow and sleete, started by pulling herself along with her hands, first on one hip then on the other until she reached the yard gate at home near ten oclock that night and called to the children but could git no answer as they was all in bed and asleep. Thinking them all massecreed she made an effort to open the gate but weak from the loss of blood flowing from both wounds she fainted and in that condition her husband found her on returning home about midnight. She was crazy or insane for a long time but under the skilful treatment of Dr. Asag, she finely recovered and lived many years before she was called to her final resting place. This band of savages kilt and scalped ten persons and scalped Mrs. Friend alive.

Now me thinks the heroism, bravery and deturmination of these three women has never been surpased in anciant or moderen history or the bravery and deturmination and example set fourth by these females ever been equeled in this age of the world.

Now nearly all of these raids was mad by Comanche Indians and nearly all mad in broad daylight. Other counties adjoining Blanco, especialy the counties north and west, suffered about the same as Blanco, but as the saying is, "let every dog shake his own tail," I shall not shake for them as I was not connected nor was I familer with but few of the outrages commited in other counties. I shall not attempt to cronical any of them except a few in Kerr and Gelispie counties which is too atrocious to leave out.

Uncle Rowland Nichols, mentioned in the firs part of this book, had emegrated to Texas about the year 1847 but lived in the eastern potion of the state until about the year 1853. He mooved to the west and after liveing around in several places he baught land and settled on the Guadaloupe River five miles above Kerrville. He was then the outside settlement. One evening comeing in from stock hunting he heard, as he thought, som turkeys gobbling and som yelping, and he told his family that he had heard a bunch of turkeys going in to the river bottom to roost and he was going to have a fat gobbler or two for break

fast and taken his gun and started off. It was now about dark
and he had not been gone long until the family heard a gun fire.
"Thare," said one, "Pa has got one."

They waited som two hours with patience, then the rest of the
night with uneasy and troubled minds. Next morning the whole
family sallied forth to serch for him, and struck his tracks and
trailed on until they found him kilt and scalped[9] but could find
no other Indian sighn but suposed by Indians, but after investi-
gating the matter closely, I have reasons to believe otherwise.

I was not in all of the scouts that followed these raiding bands
of Indians but in the most of them and when I was not with them
I had sons or friends who would give me the pertickulars in each
case. I will now return to my own history while liveing in Blanco
County.

---

[9] Bob Bennett, in *Kerr County, Texas, 1865–1956* (San Antonio: Naylor Company, 1956), p. 178, says: "Rowland Nichols, one of the earliest Kerr County settlers,
was killed by Indians in 1859. He was serving as County Commissioner at the time
of his death.'"

CHAPTER XII

Received Orders to Leave the County. Hanging Two Boys.
Robing Starrs House. Prosecuted for Killing Hogs, For Kill-
ing a Maveric, For Abuse of Stray Law, For Theft of Colt,
etc.

AFTER I TAKEN the Confederate oath the two men that
was with Col. Duff went back and reported the fact and the town
click was mad happy. A few weeks after this occurance the man
that said a Union man should not live in the county in peace
(this man was a large stock owner, had three or four hundred
head of horses on a ranch and planty of money 2,000 or 3,000
dollars and was head of the ring or click, such men wield a heavy
influance with the majority of the masses) and who we will call
head chief for short, he and the other men came up to my shop to
git some horses shod.

While thare he said, "Well, you are a good Confederate now.
You have taken the oath to suport the government."

I says, "Yes, just as good as I was before and no better, and as
I told the Col. when he come to administer the oath that I concidered a forse-put no-put a tal and it will ever be the same with
me. I shal suport the government when forsed to do so." I says
"This government [is] too corrupt to stand and it cant stand
long."

He says, "Why, [I ha]ve not seen nor heard of any corruption."

I says, "You are blind because you wont see it."

After I had finished up their work they settled up and left and
the next Saturday I was invited to attend a mass meeting gotten
up by the ring for my especial benifit but I did not attend but a
the meeting they passed resolutions to the effect that I should
leave the county in ten days or abide the consequences and appointed a commity to wait on me with a copy of these resolutions

One of them was this same head chief, another was a good friend of mine, the other a close neighbor.

Tuesday after the meeting on Satureday the three men rode up to the yard fence and hollowed and I went out and invited them down. They refused and drew out the resolutions and read them to me and said, "We are [a] commity appointed by the meeting to wait on you. What is your answer."

After they ware through I studied a few seconds [and] said, "Well, it is imposable for me to araing my buisness [so I could] leave in that short a time even if I was disposed, [and not be]ing disposed I will send in my refuseial."

One said, "I would advise you to leave, if you [do not the charges will be] so high against you they will hang you," and my friend said, "I would leave if I was in your place."

"I have done nothing to leave for and [rather] than have it said that I was run[ing away from a] mass of filthy corruption [such] as that, [I wont go if] they give me [more than] ten days."

"We have to report."

"Very well, [you can] report that if they want to hang me hey can find me right here at the end of two [dou]ble barrel shot guns.] We can git as many of you as you can of us and the irst man that crosses that fence is my meat. Now you hear my norn."

The other two turned and rode off and Callahan paused a few noments and said, "Jim, if they undertake it you shal know it n time," turned and galloped off to overtake his companions.

I worked on as though nothing had hapened but always pre-aired but heard no more from them but at the end of ten days was at home and fully prepared for any emergency. They had ried me on and I dident fit so they adopted another plan that vas to prosicute me on every pretext until they would breake me p and I would have to leave to git shet of it, which they did in he end.

I was not the only Union man in the county that they vented heir spleen upon. A few days after this they tackled old man

Starr, a thougher bred, dyed in the wool, Union man, but an ignerant, inofencive, old wore out, good easy, good nature, good for nothing kind of a fellow. He was too old to go to the ware but had three sones and three sone-in-laws that was in the right age and it was said the old man kept them hid about two miles above me on the creek and now [these civi]lized savages or heel flies, secesh, ring click, paper collar, kid glove gang of cyoties geathered togeather, 12 or 15, and went to Starrs house. He was [not there and] as they [thought] that he had gone to carry [suplies] to the son-in-laws, they interogated the family and so they caught up two of his sones, carried them down the creek interogating them whare their father was. After hanging around and could find out nothing, they ware so exasperated that they determined to make short work and went back to the house and threatened to hang the old lady if she did not tell them whare her husband was. She was over 70 years old and went half bent with age and hard work, and would not or could not give them the desired information and they commenced to rob and pillage the house. The first thing they done was to take 10 or 12 sacks of wheete that the old man had layed in for his bread and emty them out in piles for their horses to eat while they mad further serch.

The old lady had a piece of brown janes in the loom with 10 or 12 yards already wove and they cut that out. The old man had a new suit of mixed janes that he never had on, they taken them, they taken 5 new coveerlids and 4 home mad blankets they found in a teacup thirty cents in money and taken that with 5 or 6 quilts and some brass julrey. On the winde up two of the men quarreled and would have faught but for their companions interfearance about a division of the spoiles.[1]

Som of these men was Starrs close neighbors and one [of them]

---

[1] Captain J. W. Sansom, in "Memoirs in Early Texas" (unpublished manuscrip in William E. Howard Collection, D.R.T. Library, San Antonio), pp. 29, 30, give an account of similar experience at his home during this period: "The next day March 6th, I went to my home to find it taken possession of by Captain Rapp an Company of Confederate forces sent there from Austin, Texas in search of me. The were one of several such companys that had been there and there about o same business, the other companys did not disturb my family in the least. I ha been detected somewhere in route from Brazos Island and reported to General Bee headquarters at San Antonio and there kept a secret excep officers that was sent ou

was a Methodist preacher and pastor of the church and knew his three daughters and all three of his sone-in-laws went to his church. Deturmed to not be out [done they] hid themselves and watched the house until [old man Starr] returned, then serounded the house and taken him off to San Antonio and put him in jail.

Now again this blood thirsty gang of jackals turned themselves loose on old man Lundy, an old man near seventy and a criple, saying that he was hiding his sone and two or three other young men that aught to be in the servis. They arested him in order to keep him from feeding his sone and the other so they might starve in also. They still stayed out and they kept him under an arest som two weeks and finely got tired guarding him and concluded to take him to San Antonio and turn him over to the vigelence commity but when they arived, old Asa Mitchell, chairman of the commity, told them the calaboose was full and he had no room for him.

Said he, after hearing the evidence against him, "Take him up to San Pedro Springs and hang the old traitor," which they did and left him hanging and went home to Blanco.

He hung thare, it was said, until he roted down and they then commenced a vigilent serch for those young men. Then one night they was watching a house and saw two of the boys enter and they walked round unobserved to the door and Lundy was in a chier with his best girl on his lap. Two of them shot at the same time, killing Lundy so dead that he never mooved but Snow mad his escape but was [later killed in] a fight between the Union men and [this click] and, dear reader, you can understand by this [they] exicuted on every pretentes but they done with me as you will see farther on.

Then again in Agst about the 10th 1862 thare was a lot of

_____
for my capture, all of which I knew in 25 hours after General Bee did. There was a leaky vessle at his headquarters from where I got my information, so that in most cases I knew the men was coming. I had three men with me and from point of vantage saw some their movements but of course not all. They fed their horses from our barn, had our women cook for them, they wallowed the beds, sit on chairs, walke about and robed the women while cooking for them of all ther jewlry, some money, blankets, mens clothing and other things, and on leavin two saddle horses none of which was known for some time after they had left by my family."

Germans that did not want to take sides against the government of their adopted country so they held a meeting in Fredricksbourg and thirty three men agreede to leave the Confedracy and cross the Reo Granda and waite until the war was over, thare being no law to protect them in their neutrality, and after being warned to that effect by some of Col. Duffs oficers, they secretly mad preparations for their departure, collected about sixteen good wagons, good ox teams, loaded their wagons with provisions —flower, bacon and other suplies—and started for Mexico without any road. Some of Duffs men being out on a scout discovered their trail and hasened into camp and reported a large Indian trail going west and Duff ordered out Capt. Donaldson with his full company with orders to pursue the trail and if posible to overtake and kill the last one of them.

"But Col," said one of the men who had discovered the trail "the trail is made by a large outfit of wagons, horses and beef cattle and I know that it is white men and not Indians."

Now hear Col Duffs reply and notice the vindictiveness and hatred of the Union men in his orders. "It makes no difference," said he, "if it is white men shirking the servis of their coun they deserve to be treated like Indians or any other enemy. Al you have to do is to obey orders."

Two or three days after the train left Fredricksbourg, Capt John Sansom with 15 or 20 companions left the vacinity of Curry Creek settlement in Blanco County to overtake and attach them selves to the German train. They overtaken the train late in the evening near the Noesses Can[yon] at which place they all wen into camp for the night. [During the] night and next mornin Sansom urged the German[s to] organize and elect a leader urgeing the necesity of a commander in case of an attack by Indians or other enemy.

The Germans held a council in their own languege for son half hour, they suposeing that Sansom being an American saugh the command and they did not like to elect a German who nev very little of American tactics over Sansom and his men, so the told him thare was no danger as they had journied so far with

"Now you hear my horn"

out trouble. Sansom told them that he anticipated danger at any time while in Texas and that he would not travil with them unless they would organize.

They crossed over the Noeses River and took up the line of march up a long hollar or creek, traveled on until night began to set in and all went into camp, the Germans close beside a dense thicket of live oak saplins some 300 yards long, correled their wagons in front, haveing the thicket in their rear, always guarding against an atact by Indians and Sansom filed off to the left some six or seven hundred yardes on another prong of the creek. After supper they put out their fire and went to sleep.

About two hours before dawn the next morning they ware aroused by the fireing of guns. Donaldsons and his men had succeeded in crawling through the thicket and waited until that hour, then opened a heavy fire on them. The Germans rose, frightened and excited and haveing no leader ran to and fro only to be shot down like so many wolves, som fought bravely, the contest lasted until daylight when the Germans, seeing themselves sarounded, outnumbered, and overpowered, serendered.

But Donaldson had orders to not receive a serender or take any prisners, so kept up their bloody work until the last man was killed that they could find, but during the contest three of the Germans had made their escape and finely after rambling around and dodging Duffs men for two weeks, came into Fredricksbourg starved to death. Donaldsons men rounded up all the horses, cattle and oxen, picked out a good team and hitched to a large wagon that was loaded with four thousand pounds of flour, piled up the other wagons with their efects, piled all the dead bodies on the pile after rifleing them, and set fire to the pile, then mooved off with the one wagon and the stock and arived safe in camp. Duf confiscated the property and sold what they did not want to use themselves.[2]

[2] The Battle of the Nueces River, August 10, 1862, was one of the great tragedies of the Civil War in Texas. Many of the German settlers of Kerr, Kendall, and Gillespie counties remained loyal to the Union and refused to take the Confederate oath instead they vowed not to bear arms against the federal government. In the latter part of July, 1862, the counties of Kerr, Kendall, Gillespie, Edwards, and Kimbl

Sansom and his men heard the firing commence and hastely got their ponies, saddled up, mounted and rode off up the side of the mountain near a mile away and watched the issue. When all was still and they saw Doneldson and his men moove out of sight, they rode down to the camp and one of the men said in giveing me the detailes, "I never saw such a sight before in my life, and I never want to again. Fifteen wagons with their loaded efects, yoaks, saddles, blankets and the boddies of thirty men lay in one burning smokeing smoldering heap."

They gazed for a few minuts on the sickning sight, then turned and rode away. In a few days they crossed the Reo Granda and was safe. This I learned from one of Donelsons men who was a partisapant and an eye witness, and one of Sansoms men after the war closed.

Then again to show the sperit and hot blood that existed between the Confedrates and Union men I will give another item. Hiram Nelson, old man Henderson, Frank Scott, and the old man Tuerknett and half dozen others was concidered Union men or bushwhackers. They all had families dependent on them for suport, consequently, they tried to stay with them, took their families on the fronteer in the mountains in Gelispie County, lodeged around suporting themselves and families on game. But Duffs men was not to be cheated out of their prey. They followed them and hunted them down like wild beasts and finely found and captured Nelson, Scott, Henderson and Tuerknett and carried them down on Spring Creek whare thare was a large liveoake stood over a deepe hold of water and hung them to the limbs of

were placed under martial law, which Colonel James M. Duff was ordered to enforce. A group of Unionists under the command of Major Fritz Tegener decided to leave the state and go to Mexico. They were followed by Colonel Duff's company of Texas Partisan Rangers and other Partisan Ranger units, all under the command of Captain C. D. McRae of the 2nd Texas Mounted Rifles. While encamped on the Nueces River in Kinney County, Major Tegener's group was attacked by the Confederate force and forty-five of the sixty-five members were either killed in the battle or put to death after having been taken prisoner. In 1865 the remains of these men were gathered and buried beneath a monument erected in their honor at Comfort, Kendall County, Texas. See Webb and Carroll, *The Handbook of Texas*, II, 290; John W. Sansom, *Battle of Nueces River in Kinney County, Texas, August 10th, 1862* (San Antonio: n.p., 1905, 14 pages).

the trees.³ Their wives, being fearful that their husbands would
be hung, followed them, and the savages let them come close
enough to see their husbands hanging and beged to take their
boddies down and burry them but the beasts drove them off with
threats that if they came again they would put them on a limb to
dry. They taken the boddies down and threw them into the hold
of water and guarded it. In ten or twelve days the officer that had
this done was remooved and another apointed in his stid. As soon
as he took command he sent word to the women giving them
leave to burry the boddies of their husbands which they did with
great dificulty as the boddies ware so decomposed. This hapened
on the 13th of August 1863 but a little more of the same spirit
ad[d]ed, caused the savage beasts in human shape to continue
their cruelty to their fellow man. In hunting for old man Tuerknett they come across his son John, a lad of sixteen perhaps and
taken him and whiped and beat him unmercyfully, trying to
make him tell whare his father was. The boy did not know, thare-
fore could not tell and they threw him down on his back, thrus
the musel of their gun in his mouth, put their foot on his head
and prised open his mouth until they broak his under jaw, ther
tied his arms behind him and threw him into a hole of water to
drown. The man that told me of this was one of the party but said
he took no hand but they still kept up the serch for the old man
until they finely got him one evening as he and his little son, ten
or eleven years old, was going to their old place to salt their cattle
The old man certainly felt some strang forebodings for he said
"Dick, if I am kilt on this trip and you or not, recolect you mus
travel east becase thare is not settlements for a long ways west o

³ Ransleben, *A Hundred Years of Comfort in Texas*, p. 119, quotes a letter from
Howard Henderson of Ingram, Texas, to J. W. Sansom, San Antonio, dated Octobe
16, 1908, as follows: "Dear Captain:—I was in the Nueces battle, as you know, an
while reading your pamphlet account of it, could see it just as it was. . . . I am now
on my death-bed. I know that J. M. Duff and his company of murderers kille
many of my neighbors and friends. My uncle and cousins Schram Henderson, my
wife's father and brother Turknette, were murdered, my neighbors, Hiram Nelson
Frank Scott and his father, Parson Johnson and old man Scott were all butchered b
Duff and his gang. Rocks were tied to thier feet and they were thrown into Spring
Creek."

south but by traveling east you will come to the settlements first."

That night the old man was followed up and kilt and Dick carried his fathers gun and a gourd of water four days before he reached home. That was in September.

Sometime in October '63 the same party, some of Duffs men, murderd and robed old man Burk and Blank, two well-to-do German farmers liveing on South Grape Creek. They got near $16.00 in silver from the two. Two of the same purps the same summer made it a point in peachtime to visit an old Germans peach orcherd with their sacks, carrien off and wasting his fruit. The old man concluded to frighten them, saw them coming, got his double barrel shot gun, went to the orcherd and lay down, and when they came in he fired his gun, elevateing it above their heads but they wouldnt scar worth a cent. They drew their revolvers, and the old man saw them and broake to run but they pursued him firing at every jump until he reached his door whare he received two shots, fell and expired. They went back, fild their sacks and went back to camp. I could give a hundred such circumstances as the above but enough in Gelispie and Kerr Counties.

Now, dear reader, these transactions di[d not take place] out on the plains and by the wild Indians but [here in] Blanco County and amongst some few civilized peo[ple] was [it] perpetrated by this blood thirsty gang of jackalls, ring click, kid glove, paper collar beasts of prey in human shape.

In the fall old man Jacobs baught a claim or bunch of hogs and being a cripple gave me the marks and authorized me to kill all I could find in the marks on shares. I kilt some of them and the second chief claimed them and the next court I was prosicuted for heft of hogs. Of course my lawyer threw the case out but that was all they expected was to make me pay a lawyer fee and put me to as mutch trouble as possable. The next [spring] I was prosicuted or kill[ing] a mavric yearling and as they cou[ld not proove it], of course, the case was thrown out as they knew it would be but it cost me a lawyer fee which was the most and put me to trouble.

The Indians scarcely ever [went] through the county without leaveing some tired down horse on the trail. They would run them down and then abandon them or they would kill them or shoote an arrow into them or lance wound them in som way so that they could be but little or no servis to the whites for some time but the men following the trail would take them in, recruit them up and use them as their own unless the owner would call for them. This had been the ru[le] from the first settleing of Texas.

On one occaision Dick Hudson had four good poines in his possesion, at one time useing them as cow ponies. Now and then he would swap or sell one. [When he] left the county he taken off two of these horses with him. [Near]ly every man in the county knew all of this, especialy the ring town click. Montgunrey Rabl used the trail horses as they ware called and Gipson used them all togeather. When the Indians would steal his horses he would say. "Well, they got none but their own and I am not the looser." Then he would buy for a trip [from] som one who had a suply of trail ponies.

Brother John Nic[hols once when] the Indians stole his horses found they abandoned a good one [which he taken ho]me to Seguin and made property of [and he had the sa]me horse with him when he mooved [that he had] picked up on the Indian tra[i and cir]cumstances was well kno[wn to ever]yone. I mention this to show tha[t] they changed the [rule].

In following the same band that chaced Rich[ard and Fra]n Daniell, we found a mare standing in the trail in [the] same tracks where she had been abandoned the day before, hair nearly all whiped of her hind parts, shot with an arrow and lanced in the breast and about three joints of her backbone naked, the hide being worn off by rideing her barebacked. Having plenty of horse of my own, I did not care to be bothered withe her but none of the men would take her. On our return, seeing she was a good anime if in order, I attempted to drive her home, but [when] led she traveled to water, drank and let up.

A few days aft[er, I] succeeded in driveing her home, I had plenty of feede and by [treat]ing her wounds and feedeing her good she soon recovered. I did not do as the other men was doing but made all inquiry and [sent] word to all the horse men, the brands was plane, several [came] to look at her and amongst the rest the head chief of the ring but none would claim her. It went on thus for some months and I rode her when occaision required and never once thought of astraying the mare.

This man had been buisy all the time trying to find out who gave the brand and did find a man that gave one of the brands and braught him to look at the mare but he would not [claim] her. The head chief shook his head and said, "She dont belong in this part of the country so you had better estray her. [They had] their way. The next court I was indicted for abuse [of the stray] law.⁴ I beat the case as they expected but paid a la[wyers fee].

I was then indicted for removeing a hide of one of my own milk cows that died, a lawyer fee was the result and I began to realize that they would make good their threats that they would make me leave the county or send me to the penetentery. I saw that men that cared nothing for their oaths could do anything they undertook to do. I then advertised the mare in order to estray her, sent advertisements to all the adjoining counties and when one advetisement ran out I would renew.

I kept on in this way for some time when I received a leter from a man in Guadaloupe County stateing that he had seen my ad-

---

⁴ The Republic of Texas enacted laws regulating the acquistion of estrayed livestock and requiring certain procedures to be followed. In 1836 these laws governing stray animals (horses, mules, mares, colts, jacks, jennys) required the person finding the animal to go before a justice of the peace for the county and give information as to where the animal was found and what marks or brands were on it. Valuation of the animal was then made, and if no claim had been established by previous owners by the end of twelve months, the animal became the property of the person who found it. This law was amended in 1840 so that any horses or mules, etc., taken from among mustangs would not have to be legally declared estrayed but could be advertised in the nearest newspaper for thirty days and kept in the county where taken for six months. In 1863 all laws providing for the handling of estrayed stock were suspended, with the exception of those dealing with vicious or breachy animals that could cause damage to other stock or to property. See "An Act Regulating Estrays, December 22, 1836," Gammell, *Laws of the Republic of Texas*, I, 212–215; also "Section 7, Amended, Session of the 4th Congress of the Republic of Texas, February 5, 1840," *ibid.*, II, 149–151; also "Estrays, General Laws of the Extra Session of 9th Legislature of the State of Texas, February 25, 1863," Gammel, *Laws of Texas*, V, Ch. 5, p. 6.

vertisement. He stated that he gave one of the brands and that he had lost such a mare and as he was then a cripple from rheumatism if I would bring the mare down, if she was not his he would pay me for my trouble and if she was he would give me twenty dollars.

About this same time I received a letter from Alsa Miller and John Nichols to buy up all the old oxen and gentle beeves that I could and bring them down as they wanted them to fatten for market. I thought I could kill two birds with one stone as the old saying is, take the mare to the man and drive some beeves at the same time so I baught up a small bunch and mounted the mare.

I arrived at Millers late one eveing, pened the [beeves in his] pen and with Millers horses and [next m]orning all Millers horses and mules with the mare was out [and] gone and I borrowed a horse and hunted two weeks but c[ou]ld not find her. I baught a pony to ride home and the next court I was indicted for theft of stray [m]are but I put the trial off and went back, hunted [two] or three weeks more but could not find her. I offered a big reward and hired several stockmen to hunt for her and came back home and my lawyer succeeded putting the trial off for near two years, thinking I would find her, when I received a letter from James H. Putman that he had found the mare in posesion of one Jim Brown near Belmont, Gonzales County, only six miles from where I had lost her. It was no near accident that she was in an out-of-the-way pasture whare an negro man [said he] had seen her off and on for two years and a good reason for [not] finding her. She had a good yearling colt and Brown [had] branded it in his own brand and I amediately went down [and] found Brown and demanded the mare. He denied haveing such an animal and I went and got an officer and Putnam and [mad] him perduce the mare.

I says, "Whare is the colt."

He said he did not know, he had not seen it in three months. He gave the mare but not willingly and he wanted me to pay him for keepeing her so long. He wanted twenty-five dollars for his trouble but the officer told him he had better keepe quiet [for] I had the uper hand of him and I taken the mare and I went home and the next court I was ready for trial and beat the case but lost a big lawyar fee.

I then estrayed the mare and about th[is ti]me the head chief first in command concluded he [wa]s succeeding rather slow, he concluded he must have some [m]or help. He went to work and captured and imployed in his vilenaus cause the next bigest stock owner in the county. He was county clerk, a big mason, a merchent, a Methodist class leader and Sunday Scool teacher, of corse, a man of heavy influance and the two not only wielded a heavy influance but actuly ruled the county with the help of the subordents in the ring. They now set their heads togeather for my distruction and said they would run me off, break me up or send me to the penetentery. Bill Callahan was in all their meeting and caucuses and they never made a motion or threat but what I knew it soon after.

One day when I was in town the last named or second chief came to me, taken me off and stated that he had been reliable informed that the old stray mare had a colt down at Belm[ont] and that I had better go and git it, that the county would hold me responsable for the colt. I thought thare would be another lawyer fee to pay, if nothing els, and begining to find out that they could do anything they set their heads to do, I went down and demanded the colt from Brown and he gave him up without a word. I dont say that this was a trap set for me to fall into concocted by his ring and understood and assisted in by Brown but the way it worked out it showed its cloven foot mighty plain. I could neither lead nor drive the colt and broak him to ride and after remaining at home a week or two I rode the colt to town one day and the head chief claimed the colt, swore to him [before the] second in command or second chief, after telling me I had better go and git him so as to sell the colt with its mother at stray sale, and the next court I was indicted for theft of colt.

They now began to talk loud and say they had me now and would send me to the penetentery or spend the last dollar that they could both raise. Head chief told me so to my face and they now began to inlist and drill such men as they thought they could use in their buisness, some 3 or 4, and commenced to canvass the county in order to predgedis the citizens against me so when the colt case came up they would have the jury already stacked on me. They had brught in the officers too so they knew who to summons and who not to summons and now this town ring click, secesh, kid glove, paper collar, gold stud, sons of Belial had put in their work so successfully that when the colt trial came up the jury hung eleven for conviction and one for equital.

Now I will state a little of the evidence against me. The two chiefs was the main witnesses against me. They both swore about the same thing, as they had, of corse, counciled togeather and was about thus, they ware togeather on the range on Fryday evening. saw the mare, they claimed to be the mother of the colt, and she had no colt. The next Tuesday they ware out in the same range and saw the mare with a young colt and in a few days after they saw the mare without the colt and never saw the colt but the one time until they saw me rideing him the day they prooved him away from me but they both knew it was the same colt on first sight.

Now, reader, the time enterveigning between seeing the co[l:fi]rst when four days old and the time they swore to him was thr[ee] months and nine days. Now such was the greate knowledge, instinc or capassity in stockmen them days to know all the diffrent changes in color and shape that a colt four days old is subject to until it is three months old, though thare might be something in some stockmen them days that stockmen does not posses these days from a circumstance that hapened about the same time.

Another old stockman whoes name I withold and who was no interested in this colt case but was a promanent member of the Methodist Church and a half preacher swore that he had lost a mare and sucking colt unbranded. This spring A. C. Daniell had taken up and estrayed a horse and mule tied togeather the ful length of a forty feete rope. The appraisers said the horse was fourteen years old giveing full description, no brands perceive

able, etc. The Indians had stolen this old mans buggy horse sometime before and he had nothing to work, this was a ground hog
case. He takes his son-in-law, goes before the clerk and swore to
and prooved the horse to be the identical colt that he had lost fourteen years before and taken the horse and now, was not that great
knowledg, instinc or whatever it might be called, to know the
changes a colt is subject too.

After the jury hung on this colt case the judg ordered a special
venire of 60 jurrors summoned to try the case the next court.

After court adjourned the judg came to me and said, "Well,
Nichols, dont you think you can git 12 men out of 60 that will
give you justis."

I says, "Judg, I doubt it," then explained to him how they was
workeing it and the threats mad. I said, "I have many friends but
when one is sumond they always know them and objeck to
hem."

Callahan said, "The sherif too is in the intrest of the ring and
he knows your friends and will not summonds them so I doubt
ny gitting even one man on the jury so as to hang it."

The next trial the judg says, "I knew that predgedis ran high
against you but I had not drempt of such corruption."

Now during the war I was paying taxes on five hundred head
of cattle, thirty five head of horses and six hundred and fifty one
acres of as good land as thare is in Blanco County. Now in this
year 1866 I could perduse but 63 head of cattle and 13 head of
horses. Now they ware stolen from me but by whom I shal not at-
emt to say. My lawyers now began to croud me for money, I
had no stock that would sell for money and I offered my homestid
or sale. The next trial these bloodthirsty purgud mass of moove-
ng and filthy corruption had worked so industriously and spent
heir money so freely I was convicted.

Altho Brown had heard of the prossicution and sent me word to
have him summond and he would come, before the trial I
hunted him up and his brand was still on the colt plain but they
aught him or had baught him before this as he sold cheep at the
rial and he swore that he never seen the colt before and knew

nothing of the brand. I prooved by Putnam that this was the same colt that Brown had in possesion and that was the brand that Brown used on all his stock but the jury gave Putnams evidence no weight and Brown told Putnam after the trial that the ring gave him fifty dollars and expences to evade swareing the truth and that he was even with me now.

I prooved enough to have claired any other man, but it had no weight with the jury and after the trial the judg came to me and said, "You will never git a fair trial and tomorrow is motion day. You have your lawyers to moove for a new trial and a change of vinue and I will grant it."

So on the morrow the motion was mad and, of course, objected too and the lawyers spent nearly the whole day in wrangleing over it and finely late in the evening they closed their arguement and the judg granted a new trial and a change of vinue and the trial was moved to San Marcos, Hays County.

Court was some time off at that place, and my lawyers pressing me for money, I sold my place to Tom Smith of 1,000 dollars, one half money the other in trade and a few years ago Smith wa offered 10,000 dollars for the place and refused to sell. I sold wha cattle I could raise, two or three horses, and afterwards a wagon and nine yoak of oxen to Tom Johnson for 950 dollars, taken hi note, he broak, and I never received a dollar from him. I then lef Blanco County in disgust feeling like a chawed calf rope looks

I mooved into Hays County to await the ishue of my trial, but change done me no good as these hell hounds followed me to Sar Marcos with their agents and money and when the trial come of I was convicted and given five yeares in the penetentery. I taker an apeal to the Supream Court but that court would not set for month and my friends concluded that would be too long for me to lie in jail and got up a petition to the Governor for a pardor When I reached Austin I met the [Governor, got the] pardor stuck it in my pocket and struted round a month, and when th Supream Court set they reversed the judgment and now, my dea reader, heare I am yet and have never seen the inside of a pene tentiary in my life nor do I think my reputation or carecter is in jured in the least. I think my readers will agree with me that my carrecter is still unsulled and unstained. Nor do I believe with all the venomous poison that could be hurled fourth from such poluted lips at the carecter of an honest man could in the least spot, color or stain his carrecter and as they are strangers to dignity and deacency I will leave them for a while in the hands of their friends, the children of Belial, but when adversity comes through Providence, it can be meekly bourn but mans inhumanity to man makes countless thousands mourn.

In going home from the trial the head chief said to a friend of mine, "Well, we have accomplished what we set in to do, but it has cost us over three thousand dollars besides our trouble." That is prety steepe is it not to git one man out of the county.

Now, I will state that that ring click, paper collar, kid glove, gold stud, mooveing mass of filthy corruption still exists in Blanco with a few addisions and all git their sustainents by sucking the paps of the great hydreheaded monstrossity. Their lawyer still exists, a mooveing mass of filthy corruption, som have gone whare they are now sending up their fruitless cries from whare hope nor mercy never can reach them. Jim Brown is breathing out an unprofitable existance in Hays County near Dupre impatantly waiting for the devil to call for his own begotten.

Now I sometimes think of the past and how I was surved by this rotten harted, thieving, savage set of hypocritical, fraudalent, purgered and poluted set, ring click, secesh, kid glove, paper collar, brass stud, mooving mass of coruption. I say, if they could through any means escape the punishment to which their crimes so justly intitle them, then I should loose faith in an omnipotant God and wonder for what purpose hell was instituted and once more let me say, after they have sined away their day of Grace, let these erreclaimable, hardened and infamous black-mailers, sane or insane, knaves, tools or maniaces, go and regale their dubious fancies in the contemplation of their own depavity.

APPENDIX

kept out Scouts all the time when one would come in
her would go out and those that on a Scout ware every
practising horsemanship and marksmanship we put
a post about the Size of a common man then put
another about 40 yards farther on we would run our hos
full Speed and discharge our rifles at the first Post
o our Pistles and fire at the Second at first thare
Some wild Shooting but we had not Practised two
ths until thare was not many men that would not put
balls in the center of the Posts ~~then we drew~~ a ring at
the Size of a mans head and Soon every man could
t his balls in the circle we would Practice this awhile
try rideing like the comanche Indians after Practis
or three or four months we became so Purfect that we
ld run our horses half or full Spade and Pick up a
a coat a blanket or rope or even a Silver dollar Stan
n the Saddle git behind it jump to the ground and bac
The Saddle throw our Selves ~~on the~~ Side of our horses with
a foot and a hand to be Seen and Shoot our Pistols and
te horses neck rise up and reverse &c at one time being
Down at Some Pony races Calvin. Turner and myself
d to bet ten dollars that either of our horses could
any Saddle horse in Down and we would ride Standing
te Saddle we could not git a bet and in the even
him and I ran our horses through the track about
Speede Standing in the Saddle we had just been out
sing and went in to camp when Some of the boys discover
n rideing at a breakneck gate coming directly towards
n arriveing he Says Indians boys he said thare was 30 or 40

A page from the Journal.

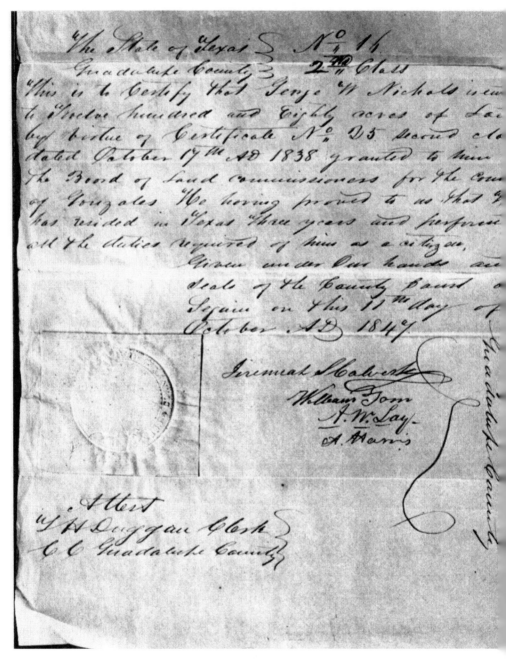

*Second-Class Headright issued October, 1847, to George W. Nichols,
father of James W. Nichols.*

Republic of Texas
County of Gonzales } Know all men by these presents that on the 2nd day of May One Thousand and Eight hundred & thirty eight, that John W. Nichols, applied for a Licens to authorize any lawful person to solemnize the Bonds of Matrimony between him the said John W. Nichols & Polly M. Day both of the County & Republic afsd. This is therefore to authorize any legal person to marry the said John W. Nichols & Polly M. Day, in conformity with the Fourth Section of the act authorizing the marriage of persons in this Republic, and the person so solemnizing marriage will endorse the same on this Licens and make return to this office that the same may be placed on record according to law, there being no seal of office this the day and Given under my hand and private seal date above written

Ezekiel Williams County Clerk
for the Cty of Gonzales

1arriage license issued May 2, 1838, to John Nichols, brother of Jim Nichols, and Polly M. Day, a neighbor girl.

Republic of Texas
County of Gonzales

Know all men by these presents that William W. Allsberry as principal and Isom J. Good as security are held and firmly bound in the sum of Three Thousand Dollars payable to the president of the aforesaid Republic or his successors in office.

The condition of the above obligation is sutch that whereas the afforesaid William W. Allsberry and Sarah Madissa Day both of the Republic and County aforesaid have consented and agreed to live together as man and wife in lawful wedlock as will appear by license granted to the aforesaid Allsberry and Sarah M. Day by Ezekiel Williams Clerk of the County Court of the aforesaid County. Know therefore know ye that if the aforesaid William W. Allsberry and Sarah M. Day shall wed and truly comply with the foregoing obligation then and in that case the instrument shall be null and void, otherwise remain in full force and effect, this the fifteenth day of April A.D. Eighteen hundred and thirty eight.

Wm. W. Alsbury
I. J. Good

Signed in presence of
John C. Hunt
J. D. Clements

Marriage bond for $3,000 to secure the marriage between William W. Allsberry and Sarah M. Day, April 15, 1838. The marriage bond was often used on the frontier in place of a marriage ceremony.

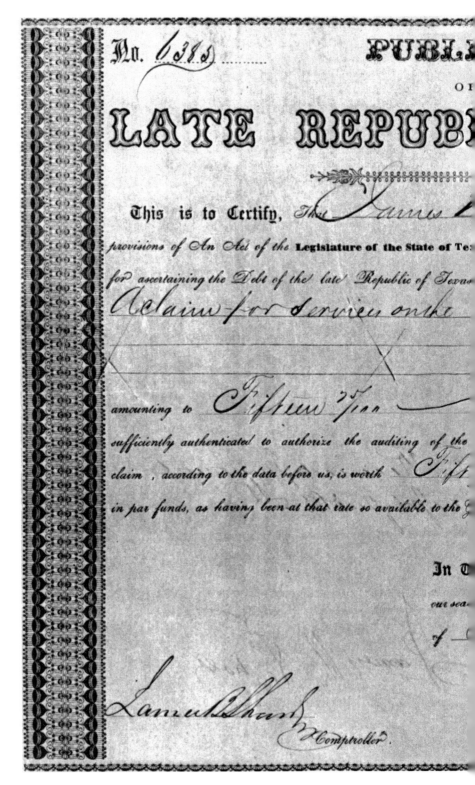

№. *6385* **PUBLI**

OF

LATE REPUBL

This is to Certify, *The James*

provisions of An Act of the **Legislature of the State of Te:**

for ascertaining the Debt of the late Republic of Texas

A claim for services on the

amounting to Fifteen 75/100

sufficiently authenticated to authorize the auditing of the

claim, according to the data before us, is worth Fif

in par funds, as having been at that rate so available to the

In C

our sea

of

Samuel Shaw

Comptroller.

Acknowledgment by "The Late Republic of Texas" of a $15 debt out

Woll, a Mexican leader who captured and held San Antonio for a o

Nichols _____ has, under the

An Act to extend the provisions of "An Act to provide

uary 7, 1853, filed with the **Auditor and Comptroller,**

Campaign in 184 2

_____ *Dollars; which is*

the laws of the late Republic of Texas. Said

_____ *Dollars,*

)hereof, We have hereunto set our hands and affixed

Austin, this 2_ *day*

_____ *A. D. 1855*

Jn? N. Miller(?)

Auditor.

hols for his services in the campaign against General
fter Texas had won its independence from Mexico.

Gonzales County 1869 map shows early townsite of Gonzales near juncture of San Marcos River and Guadalupe River. Jim Nichols' holding (outlined in lower left corner) is northwest of townsite, near San Marcos River.

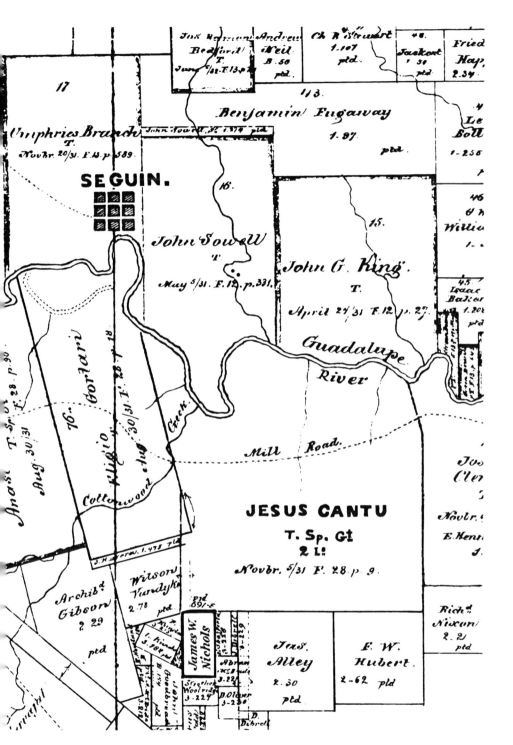

Guadalupe County 1869 map shows tiny Seguin townsite on winding Guadalupe River. Jim Nichols' holding (outlined in lower left) is south of Mill Road.

Blanco July 9th 1868

His Excellency the Governor of Texas

I am Ordered by the Honorable Police Court now in Session at Blanco To inform you That of an Indian Raid in this and Cannal County

The Indians Variously Estimated at from 25 to 50 in Number Came down the Guadaloupe River (as is Supposed) the first that was Seen of them was about 15 or 20 miles due South of Blanco C.H. at least 20 miles farther into the Settlements than they have been known to come for 15 years an yesterday morning the Bodys of Mr. W S Shepherd and his wife (a daughter of Mr. N.W. Huckabee) and the Child of Mr. Shepherd was found dead murdered & Scalped an the trail of the Indians the Body were Striped & the Childs head cut off & found Some distance from its body The bodys had lain from Thursday noon until yesterday monday noon about 7 miles South East of Blanco Court House Mr. Shepherd had been Shot with a Rifle or Six Shooter Through the body Mrs Shepherd was Shot with two arrows in the back one Coming in the breast There is also a Son of Mr. Huckabee about 14 or 15 years that was with Shepherd & formerly that is either killed or been carried

*A report to the State of Texas about Indian depredations
committed in Blanco County between 1865–1870.*

INDEX

Lightning Source UK Ltd.
Milton Keynes UK
UKOW03f0615120614

233274UK00001B/101/P